KINGS OF
THE INTERNET

What you Don't Know about them ?

MOHAMMAD BAHARETH

iUniverse, Inc.
Bloomington

Kings of the Internet, First Edition

Part of the iSay Franshise

ISBN-13 978-1-4697-9842-4 (sc)
ISBN-13 978-1-4697-9843-1 (ebk)

Author:
Mohammad Bahareth
www.Bahareth.info

Design:
Mohammad AbuEyada
abu3yada@gmail.com | facebook.com/h4design.net

Warning and Disclaimer:
Every effort has been made to make this book s complete and accurate as possible, but no warranty or fitness is implied. the information provid-ed is on an "as is" basis. The Author And the Publisher shall have neither liability nor responsibility to any person or entity with respect to any loss or damages arising from the information contained in this book.

Contents

INTRODUCTION

From Just-another-idea to a Million-Dollar-internet-phenomenon

Don't know what it means, no problem, 'just google it' . . . Feeling bored? Check out what your friends are planning . . . Want to cook something special to impress your loved one, but don't know how to do that? Well, if you have a computer then you have an answer to all your queries. Yes, the word is "Internet". Internet has made it possible to bring the entire virtual world at your fingertips. Now, it is not just a means of entertainment, but it has become a part of our daily life, we can also say that it has become a necessity.

There are a lot of great personalities in the world who always inspired our life in many different ways with the different qualities they possesses in which they have excelled in their life. Some of them have their great inventions that have revolutionized our world. Others have liberated nations by gaining freedom for the people. Some have amazed us with their fascinating art. Others have given us insight as to how we should live a happy life. Some have dedicated their life for helping others. Some have conquered mountain peaks while others have established business empires. Some are great poets and writers while others have mesmerized us with their brilliant melodies.

We all learned a lot from these people by studying what they said, what they did and applying their lessons and wisdom to our own lives. Here is a list of individuals who have made our lives easier by bring the whole world into one desk, by transforming a simple idea in their mind into billion dollar business.

They just changed the way we think, we interact and we do things in our day-to-day life. They not only built their business empires but also brought huge business for their country. They not only earned billion dollars of their own but also created thousand of employments for the techno savvy youths all over the world. They customized the high end cutting edge technology into a recipe which can be served in the breakfast, lunch and dinner table of every common man.

Internet is considered among one of those inventions of modern age which have just revolutionized the world. It's the most powerful & versatile source of knowledge for every common man today. It has touched every aspect of our life. Be it some delicate medical condition, be it decorating your home and diet of your loving pets, be it finding the whereabouts of one of your dearest friend of your school, be it a very personal problem in your life and many more; information pertaining to anything and everything that we can think of, can be obtained through Internet.

In this book, we will be introduced with the masterminds who were behind the idea of creating a world at the back of a monitor screen. From just an idea, they have created technology that has brought about a difference in our lives. They who made our life easier by making our day to day work just a few click away. They who brought us close to our dear ones. They are referred to the "Kings of Internet". They are the ones who took the technology to common hands with the powerful tools they have invented and transformed Internet into a huge market place. Here we are trying to honor those Kings with few sentences on their early life, their struggle, the achievement they have made and their future plan for us.

Sergey Brin,
Co-Founder of Google

When it comes to searching for a piece of inarticulate information in the great ocean of information for a common man, Google acts like the life board to take him to his destination surely & safely. When it comes to solving the puzzle of a complex computer language for a computer programmer, Google is like the best friend seating aside helping him all through his task. When it comes to the knowledge hunger scholars who have endless thirst for the knowledge, Google proved to be the best source of knowledge for any subject that exists in this world. Yes, now google is not just the name of a site it has become a part of the dictionary, where google means search.

It's about the famous garage in Menlo Park where world's biggest internet company, Google Inc started its operation with few rented internet servers. It's about the dream and dedication of two students of Stanford who used to fight on most of the intellectual subjects and later on became intellectual soul-mates. It's about the courage of two friends who had the guts to suspend their PhD studies and created world's best internet search engine.

Sergey Mikhaylovich Brin, the Co-Founder of Google was born on August 21, 1973 in Moscow to Jewish parents. He is a Russian American computer Scientist and a legendary industrialist. He co-founded the world's largest internet company Google, along with one of his friends Larry Page. According to the estimates of 2011, Brin's personal wealth is estimated to be 19.8 billion dollars.

At the delicate age of six, Brin emigrated from Russia to the United States. He completed his undergraduate degree from University of Maryland. He followed the footsteps of his father and grandfather by studying computer science and mathematics. His father Michael Brin is a mathematics professor at the University of Maryland and mother Eugenia Brin a research scientist at NASA's Goddard Space Flight Center.

"Life is not always a Bed of Roses" appeared to be true for Sergey's father Mr. Michael Brin and his family. They had to suffer a lot in their home land Russia before they immigrated to United States because of anti-Semitism policies of communist party in Russia. His father Michael Brin compelled to abandon his dream to become an astronomer as Jews were not allowed to pursue higher studies in certain subjects like Physics and were deprived of pursuing studies in certain high ranked universities in Russia.

Michael Brin, therefore decided to study mathematics and he proved to be a genius in the field of mathematics. The thought of immigrating from Russia to United States got into his mind when he participated in the mathematics conference in Warsaw, Poland in the year 1977 where he got an opportunity to share ideas and thoughts with the greatest mathematicians from US, UK, Germany and France and soon he realized that his family will have a better future and freedom in those countries than in Russia and also their miseries due to political exploitation in the country will come to an end.

After he came back from conference in Warsaw (Poland), he decided to emigrate from Russia to United States. Although Sergey's mother was not at all willing to leave their small home in Moscow where they have all their memories of life but his father had to take a firm decision considering his son's future.

Despite all hurdles, Michael Brin applied for the exit visa for his family in the year 1978 even though he was not sure whether he will get the visa or not and it can have very adverse repercussion. Prejudicially as soon it came to Russia Government's notice, they fired him from his job and in another few days fired his wife from her job. Next couple of months till they got an exit visa, his family went through a miserable life with immense financial crisis. Finally they got the official visa to leave the country in 1979 and immigrated to United States when Brin was six years old.

The Brins took a rented house at Maryland in a very ordinary middleclass colony for his family to stay. They enrolled Sergey in Paint Branch Montessori School in Adelphi, Maryland. Michael Brin struggled to get a job of a professor in the Department of Mathematics, at University of Maryland and slowly their life started coming to normalcy.

Apart from Sergey's studies at school his father used to teach him mathematics and computer programming and his mother used to teach him Russian language. After completing his High School studies from Eleanor Roosevelt High School in Greenbelt, Maryland, he joined the University of Maryland, College Park for his Bachelor's degree where he received a Bachelor degree in mathematics and computer science in May 1993 with honors.

He began his study for graduation in Computer Science at Stanford University where he met Larry Page, his friend, intellectual soul-mates, the other Co-Founder of Google Inc. In the initial days they did not get along with each other very well, they always disapproved of each other and thereby apparently they spent most of their time arguing with one another. However, one fine day they agreed on one very interesting topic of searching and sorting out relevant information from the vast internet which was again part of their research paper entitled "The Anatomy of a Large-Scale Hyper textual Web Search Engine". They also developed and tested their new search engine designs for web in their dormitory room with few inexpensive computers.

Once they were convinced that the new search engine is successful they began to look around for interested parties to sell their search engine but surprisingly no one was interested to buy it amongst the major Internet companies of that time as they could not realize the potential of what the duo had created. Finally Sergey & Larry designed a business plan to start their own company called Google; now Google Inc, the world's biggest internet company. The name Google derived from the word 'googol' which stands for the number 1 followed by 100 zeros.

Sergey & Larry somehow accumulated some money from their family and friends to buy few cheap servers and rent that famous garage in Menlo Park to start operation of their new company. Interestingly, few months after the initiation of Google, they received a cheque of $100,000 in the name of "Google, Inc." from the co-founder of Sun Microsystems but they were not able to deposit the cheque for about two weeks as "Google, Inc." did not yet existed; the company hadn't been incorporated then. The duo then managed to complete the paperwork for two weeks and finally "Google, Inc." was officially registered and they were able to deposit the money in its account.

Apart from managing the "Google, Inc." and the decision making responsibilities of the great Organization, Brin and Page are involved in many other projects, for example, they, through Google.org are trying to help solve the world's energy and climate problems and help alternative energy industry to find wider sources of renewable energy.

Brin received many awards and recognitions for his remarkable contributions in the field of Information Technology & Engineering. In 2009, Forbes magazine declared Brin and Larry Page as the fifth most powerful people in the world. In the same year Brin was inducted into the National Academy of Engineering, which is among the highest professional distinctions accorded to an engineer.

In 2003, both Brin and Page received an honorary MBA from IE Business School for their entrepreneurial spirit and lending momentum to the creation of new businesses. In 2004, they received the Marconi Foundation Prize, the Highest Award in Engineering and were elected Fellows of the Marconi Foundation at Columbia University. In 1999, Google received the Technical Excellence Award for Innovation in Web Application Development.

In 2000, Google received Webby Award, a People's Voice Award for technical achievement. In 2001, Google was awarded Outstanding Search Service, Best Image Search Engine, Best Design, Most Webmaster Friendly Search Engine and Best Search Feature at the Search Engine Watch Awards. According to Forbes magazine Brin and Larry Page are currently together as the 24th richest person in the world with a personal wealth of US$17.5 billion in 2010.

As per his personal life is concerned, Brin got married to Anne Wojcicki in The Bahamas, in May 2007. Anne is a biotech analyst. She graduated with B.S. in Biology from the Yale University in the year 1996. She is very much interested in health information, and together with Brin they are developing new ways to develop access to it. They have put much effort in brainstorming with the leading researchers regarding the human genome project. They together started a new project on genetics and computing which will help people to know their genetic code and possibly many of the genetic problems could be corrected.

Eugenia, Brin's mother was diagnosed with Parkinson's Disease. His mother was being treated in the University of Maryland of Medicine. In 2008, Brin decided to donate funds where his mother was being treated. By using the services of 23andMe, Brin was able to discover that though the Parkinson's Disease was not hereditary, yet there are chances of him getting this disease in the later years of his life. It is due to the process of mutation of the LRRK2 gene that both his mother and Brin have in common, that increases the chances of Parkinson's disease by 20-80%. Brin considered the disease to be a bug in his system, and explained that in the same way as bugs are removed from the computer, this disease will get cured by proper treatment.

Google reported a large cyber attack on its corporate infrastructure and computers on January 12, 2010, including access to numerous Gmail accounts as well as the burglary of Google's intellectual property. It was later discovered that the attack originated in China. Google immediately took the decision to no longer censor the site in China and would completely exit from the country as a whole. As reported by The New York Times, the main aim of the attackers was to access the Gmail account of the human rights activist of China. But along with that the attackers also aimed at several large companies in the technology, finance, chemical and media sector.

While keeping its uncensored Hong Kong site in operation, Google officially discontinued its China based search engine in late March, 2010. In an interview Brin stated that he is glad that the service of Google is stopped in China, as the country was influencing other countries to create a barred censor in the process of information, and Google does not want to restrict the openness of the site, which will limit the freedom of information on the Internet.

Brin's step was quite appreciated by the U.S. Government. And it was considered to be a wise and bold step taken in the favor of freedom of speech and expression. Brin stated in an interview while speaking for Google that, "One of the reasons I am glad we are making this move in China is that the China situation was really emboldening other countries to try and implement their own firewalls."[1] While with an interview with *Spiegel*, he added, "For us it has always been a discussion about how we can best fight for openness on the Internet. We believe that this is the best thing that we can do for preserving the principles of the openness and freedom of information on the Internet."[2]

Brin's effort towards the freedom of Information and his endeavor to spread knowledge all around the world has set a milestone for the future generation to follow.

Google is not the only thing Brin is associated with. His farsightedness and will to bring changes in the world has not ended yet. He in association with Page, are finding new ways to solve the global problem of climate and energy through Google's philanthropic arm Google.org, the organization created by the duo which invests in the <u>alternative energy</u> industry to find the wider sources of renewable energy. Their main aim behind these inventions is to solve big problems with the help of technology.

Despite being so successful, Brin still maintains the same punctuality and enthusiasm at his work as it was during his initial days at Google. He maintains the same devotion towards his work as he used to do and even more. He considers hard work and dedication as the mantra for success, which is a paradigm for other employees. He is definitely one of the Kings of the Internet.

---

[1] http://online.wsj.com/article/SB100014240527487042665045751410642
     59998090.html
[2] http://www.spiegel.de/international/business/0,1518,686269,00.html

Larry Page, Co-Founder of Google

Great things happen easily when great peoples get associated. Probably humanity would not have such a great invention like Google search engine if Larry Page, Co-Founder of Google would not have met Sergey Brin, the other Co-Founder in Stanford University during their induction program. These two inquisitive minds kept aside their PhD studies and were in search of a search engine which can produce the exact search results from the vast World Wide Web.

Lawrence "Larry" Page was born on March 26, 1973 in East Lansing, Michigan. His father, Carl V. Page and his mother were computer science professors at Michigan State University. Dr. Page was a pioneer in computer science and artificial intelligence research and was one of the first faculty members of the department of computer science and engineering at Michigan State University. He received his PhD in computer science from the University of Michigan in 1965. After teaching at the University of North Carolina at Chapel Hill, he joined the MSU faculty in 1967. Although Larry Page is Jewish on his mother's side but he was raised without any religious belief.

Page completed his schooling from Okemos Montessori School Michigan in 1979 and did high school from East Lansing High School in 1991. After school, he did his Bachelor of Science degree in computer engineering from the University of Michigan with honors and a Masters degree in computer science from Stanford University.

This mastermind had a strong desire for doing new inventions from his school and college days. He was a bright kid always fascinated with computers and science magazines. He created an inkjet printer during his college days. Apart from computer studies he also had strong inclination towards astrophysics and was a member of University of Michigan Solar team.

During his PhD. program in computer science at Stanford University, Larry Page was doing a research on the mathematical properties of the World Wide Web, analyzing its link structure as a huge graph. His supervisor in the university, Terry Winograd encouraged him to continue his exploration in this field and so he began focusing on studying the way web pages were linked to other pages. Sergey Brin soon joined his research project named "BackRub" in March 1995 who was also a PhD student at Stanford.

When they started this project, there were approximately 10 million web pages available in the World Wide Web and innumerable hyperlinks. Among them and the computing resources' requirement to search for something specific in particular in the web was huge. Unaware of the fact Page & Brin began building out their crawler for the search engine and despite immense complexity of the project they succeeded to build up the basic version of the search engine.

With the basic search engine in hand they gradually started developing the algorithm for ranking a web page compared to its competitors to measure its relevance and importance for a specific search criteria. And thus, Google search engine took birth in their common dormitory room and both of them tested its efficiency for web with few cheap computers. Once the search engine was tested successfully, initially they began to look around for interested parties to sell it but surprisingly no one was interested to buy it amongst the major Internet companies of that time as they could not realize the potential of the amazing engine. Finally Sergey & Larry designed a business plan to start their own company called Google; now Google Inc, the world's biggest internet company.

Larry took the responsibility of chief executive officer of Google Inc. He was the first CEO of the company and performed his responsibilities until 2001 growing the company to more than 200 employees and a huge profitability. He was responsible for Google's day to day operations as well as leading the company's product development and technology strategy.

Larry & Brin nurtured the Google web site and the company in a completely different way unlike the conventional companies in the web site business. Google's site design and advertising strategy was completely different. It's a user friendly and simple search interface. No pop-up windows or banner ads were used, a very plainly designed homepage offered little more than the Google logo and a single search box.

Google's office culture is entirely unique where work satisfaction for the employees is one of the highest priorities. Here every employee of the company gets a chance to do something of their own interest, and the management always encourages innovative ideas. Google News, Google Maps, Google Earth, Gmail and many more are few of those innovations. Google management believes in clean and ethical ad business and encourages its business partners, vendors to demonstrate the same.

Apart from performing his responsibilities at Google, Page is also involved in helping alternative energy companies through Google.org, Google's philanthropic arm and also one of the vibrant investors in those companies like Tesla Motors which developed the Tesla Roadster, a 244-mile (393 km) range battery electric vehicle. Larry & Brin have also produced a film in 2007 named Broken Arrows.

Page married Lucinda Southworth at Necker Island in 2007. She is a research scientist. She is also sister of model and actress, Carrie Southworth. They got married at Necker Island, a Caribbean island belonging to Richard Branson. They have one child. Page is a very family oriented person and always gives it a high importance. In one of his speech at Stanford University he says about his father Dr. Carl Page who was always a teacher, a mentor, and a best friend to him—

> *"If my Dad was alive today, the thing I think he would be most happy about is that Lucy and I have a baby in the hopper. I think he would have been annoyed that I hadn't gotten my Ph.D. yet (thanks, Michigan!). Dad was so full of insights, of excitement about new things, that to this day, I often wonder what he would think about some new development. If he were here today—well, it would be one of the best days of his life. He'd be like a kid in a candy store. For a day, he'd be young*

again. Many of us are fortunate enough to be here with family. Some of us have dear friends and family to go home to. And who knows, perhaps some of you, like Lucy and I, are dreaming about future families of your own. Just like me, your families brought you here, and you brought them here. Please keep them close and remember: they are what really matters in life." [3]

Brain and Page was awarded honorary MBA degree by IE Business School for embodying the entrepreneurial spirit and lending momentum to the creation of new businesses in the year 2003. In 2004 they received the Marconi foundation prize, the highest award in engineering and were elected fellows of the Marconi foundation at Columbia University. They were declared world's most influential communications technology pioneers in year 2004. Page was elected to the National Academy of Engineering in 2004. Page and Brin were elected Fellows of the American Academy of Arts and Sciences.

In 2002 the World Economic Forum named Page a Global Leader of tomorrow and in 2004 the X PRIZE chose Page as a trustee for their board. In 1999 PC Magazine declared Google as among the Top 100 Web Sites and Search Engines and awarded Google the Technical Excellence award for innovation in web application development. In 2000 Google earned a Webby Award, a People's Voice award for technical achievement and was awarded outstanding search service, best image search engine, best design, most webmaster friendly search engine, and best search feature at the search engine watch awards. In 2009 Page received an honorary doctorate from the University of Michigan and in 2004 Page and Brin were named "Persons of the Week" by ABC World News Tonight.

Page's personal wealth is estimated to be $19.8 billion as of 2011. He was ranked 24th on the Forbes list of the world's billionaires and as the 11th richest person in the United States in 2011. This person along with his friend completely revolutionized the world of information by giving everybody, access to everything on the Internet. He deserves the title of the king of the internet.

---

[3]   http://sandeshkumar.com/2011/04/page/2/

MARK ZUCKERBERG—FOUNDER OF FACEBOOK

Few people are born to create a revolution with their path breaking ideas. They develop something unprecedented that brings a massive change in the way of living for common people. Mark Zuckerberg is one of them who have enlisted his name in hall of fame of Information Technology. He made a remarkable change in the way people interact by developing social networking site Facebook. Billions of people across the world are connected to each other and communicating endlessly through this site at the comfort of their home or during busy schedule at office without any hassle. Zuckerberg was awarded Time magazine's person of the year in 2010. He accumulated a total personal wealth of $13 billion at the age of just 27.

Mark Elliot Zuckerberg is not only a computer programmer and internet entrepreneur, he is a leading business personality who has gone into Forbes billionaire list and made his company, Facebook, entered into Fortune 500 list. The social outcry and massive demonstration at Tunisia, Egypt and Libya was possible by creating social movement through sites like Facebook. Zukerberg was a prodigy in his early life. He started dealing with computers and making software while he was in middle school. His father was his first mentor who familiarized with him BASIC programming way back in 1990s and later on a tutor with name David Newman had been assigned to hone his skill in computer science.

He was so inclined towards computer programming and language learning that Zuckerberg undertook a graduate course in the subject at Mercy College close to his home irrespective of being a student at high school. He was engrossed in developing computer programs, especially communication tools and games. He even helped his father's dental practice operated from their home through the setup program. He crafted a software program called "ZuckNet," which enabled all the computers between the house and dental office to interact with each other. It later came in the form of AOL's Instant Messenger. At the time while Zuckerberg was in high school, he configured a music player named Synapse Media Player that used artificial intelligence to understand the user's listening habits. Synapse became a huge success and Microsoft and AOL was in race to secure Synapse and take Zuckerberg in their payroll. But he didn't get carried away with such tantalizing offer and in September 2002 he joined Harvard College.

In Harvard also his glory remained unabated. He maintained his gusto and earned recognition like "Programming Prodigy". He studied psychology and computer science and joined a Jewish group with name 'Alpha, Epsilon Pi' which served as a platform for the young talent. He was acclaimed to develop a program named Coursematch which helped students to prepare their lesson. But his creativity went through rough weather when he made Facemash where visitors had to vote sensual classmate and give them ranking.

Funfilled site became a craze and its popularity exceeded the capacity of server and finally it was shut down. Zuckerberg earned a bad name because of using classmates' photo without their consent. His site was condemned for being improper and he had to apologize in public. But this event was a boon in disguise. He envisaged the strength and shortcomings of the site. He thought if Harvard University is not going to do anything about it, he will do it himself to give an opportunity to students at large to upload their personal data and interact with likeminded pupil.

Finally his idea saw the light of the day when he initiated Facebook from his Harvard Dormitory room. The inspiration invoked from Phillips Exeter Academy wherefrom he graduated in 2002. What was actually student's own directory in the form of "The photo address book", gained popularity in the name of "The Facebook".

This site became an instant hit as students had been looking forward to typical site with all relevant attributes necessary for socializing and updating personal details without much apprehension. It was initially a 'Harvard thing' but Zuckerberg with the help of his roommate Dustin Moskovitch spread its circumference to encompass Stanford, Dartmouth, Columbia, New York University, Cornell, Brown, and Yale, and then at other schools as well that had social affiliation with Harvard. With the business plan in his mind, Zuckerberg migrated to Palo Alto, California, with Moskovitz and other friends. He first set up his office over there without caring to return to Harvard. The major corporations showed interest in their business and offered hefty amount but Zuckerberg didn't respond to such temptations and remained steadfast in his mission of creating an open information flow for people. Facebook never faced financial stringency but the founder didn't hesitate to take advice from topnotch honcho like former Netscape CFO Peter Currie about financing tactics for Facebook.

Zuckerberg explained the reason of him turning down the offers, in an interview that took place in the year 2007. He explained that, "It's not because of the amount of money. For me and my colleagues, the most important thing is that we create an open information flow for people. Having media corporations owned by <u>conglomerates</u> is just not an attractive idea to me." [4]

Facebook's popularity grew by leaps and bounds and user base became 500 million by the end of July, 2010. When there was the scope of earning plenty of money through advertising as Facebook has experienced phenomenal growth, it remained contended with only selling of 10 percent of website page to keep its user happy and allow them to use more space to feed in more data and decorate page to user's heart content. In 2010, Steven Levy, the author of the book Hackers: Heroes of the Computer Revolution(1984), got angry with Zuckerberg as he thought him to be involved in hacking materials and got into infringement of law. In an answer to that, Zuckerberg said that "it's OK to break things—to make them better." Zuckerberg put his heart and soul into his social networking site and worked relentlessly to upgrade its standard and made it useful for all and sundry.

His celebrity status gained strength to strength and his rank rose from 23 to 1 in the list of Vanity Fair top 100 "most influential people of information age" in the time span of 2009 to 2010. He was even nominated as 16th in

---

[4]   http://www.exeter.edu/news_and_events/news_events_5594.aspx

"Fifty most influential figure" by New Statesman in 2010. Zuckerberg's recognition was not limited to his rank in Forbes, Vanity Fair or Times magazine most influential people in the year list. A full-fledged motion picture 'The Social Network' was made to commemorate creativity of the Facebook founder. The movie was released in October 1, 2010 and went to be a sensational hit across the world. The film secured its topmost position in many critics' list of the best film of 2010 such as 'The New York Times', 'Washington Post', 'The Wall Street Journal'. 'The Social Network' has amassed $22.4 million in 2711 theatre in the opening weekend of movie release in US. The movie received 8 nominations for Academy Awards including Best Picture, Best Actor, Best Cinematography, Best Director, Best Film Editing, Best Original Score, Best Sound and Best Adapted Screenplay and finally won three at the 83rd Academy Awards held on February 27, 2011.

Similar to any other website, Facebook too was not devoid of controversies. In the same way, as the site grew in size and number, the controversies related to the site grew at a same pace. The social networking site had to deal with a number of criticisms on different concerns including child safety, online privacy, and the inability to cease the accounts without manually deleting the content first. Both on and off the site, there have been several issues relating to the controversial issues, discussions and forums, being displayed on the site.

Three of the Harvard students, Tyler Winklevoss, Divya Narendra and Cameron Winklevoss, indicted Zuckerberg with the charges of intentionally forcing them to believe that he would assist them in building the social network called HarvardConnection.com, which was afterwards created and named as ConnectU. In 2004, they filed a law suit against Zuckerburg related to these charges, but the case was dismissed on March 28, 2007, due to some technicalities. But the case was refilled in the federal court in Boston. But Facebook filed a counter suit against the Social Butterfly, which was a project that was created by The Winklevoss Chang Group, which was an alleged partnership between i2hub and ConnectU. The case settled on June 25, 2008, and consequently, Facebook had to pay $20 million in cash and transfer more than 1.2 million common shares to the Ex-classmates of Zuckerburg.

Over the year, Mark Zuckerberg has reached stardom level and made his permanent place over there. He is role model for millions of youngsters who are influenced by the angel looking computer programmer's astounding success story. Zuckerberg has walked past many milestones in his venture to be successful entrepreneur. He had been awarded as 2007 Crunchie Award for 'Best Startup CEO'. He is also sharing seats with eminent personality such as Bill Gates and Steve Jobs in technology domain while he has been nominated as 'Simpsons' Cameo in April 2010. It is still wonder for many how a Harvard dropout fellow has made a remarkable progress in highly competitive world where he has to deal with heavyweight opponents such as Twitter, LinkedIn etc and went on to be a billionaire at young stage of life. The founder, CEO and Board of Directors has many more ventures ahead where he will display his unflinching courage, unequivocal creativity and unbridled commitment. He is definitely one of Kings of the internet.

Jack Dorsey, Founder of Twitter

The most important thing in business is the vision to see things differently and the passion to connect your idea to the people who will benefit from it. Jack Dorsey, the founder of Twitter had that vision and the passion to transform his simple idea into worlds most popular and powerful information network. Jack Dorsey, creator of Twitter, an American software architect was born on November 19, 1976. Dorsey grew up in St. Louis, Missouri.

He completed his schooling from Bishop DuBourg High School and attended Missouri University of Science and Technology and later joined New York University where he first envisioned the idea for Twitter. Before completing his degree from New York University, he moved to Oakland, California in 2000 where he started a company which offers dispatch logistics services.

From the adolescent age of just 13, he was interested in dispatch routing. Before Twitter, Dorsey's focus was to develop dispatch software to track ambulances and taxis to visualize their current status. For that he used to create a number of open source software in the area of dispatch logistics which were used widely by taxicab companies. He had several other ideas and projects in his mind as well, which included networks of medical devices along with a "frictionless service market". While working on dispatch logistics the idea of Twitter came to his mind.

Just after starting his company, Dorsey came up with the idea for a site that would combine the dispatch software with instant messaging. With that idea in mind Dorsey, Stone and Odeo, the co-founder Evan Williams, started a new company called Obvious which later evolved into Twitter. Within couple of days, Dorsey had built a simple site where users could instantly post short messages of 140 characters known as "tweets".

Jack Dorsey posted the world's first tweet on March 21, 2006 and he took the responsibility of chief executive officer of the company. He carried out the responsibility for approximately two years and in 2008, Co-founder Evan Williams replaced Dorsey as Twitter's CEO and Dorsey became the chairman of the company.

Twitter quickly attracted popularity, something much more than a messaging or friend tracking service. It became a medium for reporting experiences to highly connected audiences. One message and suddenly the whole world has access to that Tweet, this turned out to be really stunning for people.

Dorsey's idea for Twitter is also transformative. In a way, it is not designed to be a social network, but instead it serves as a raw utility. It was unique in terms of how people approached and defined it. People could report about the earthquakes they just felt, what they had for breakfast, and each time they Tweet, it sparks interaction.

Although Twitter suffered few setbacks during its early days but later on proved to be a very powerful tool in different occasions. Twitter became a powerful platform for U.S. President Barack Obama during his election campaign. Twitter also vaulted to international prominence during presidential elections in Iran. In 2010, Twitter had more than 105 million users who together tweeted some 55 million times a day. Apart from his Twitter, Dorsey is also an active investor in the social networking company, Foursquare and launched a new venture, Square, which allows people to receive credit card payments through a tiny device plugged in to their mobile phone or computer.

The device is a small square-shaped object that has the ability to be attached to devices such as an iPhone, iPad or Android device through the headphone jack. This product is a mini card reader, which allows a person to swipe their card, choose an amount to give to the recipient and then sign their name for confirmation. Square is also a system for sending paperless receipts via text message or email. Although Twitter has already revolutionized the way people communicates but Dorsey believes that still some advancement in some features is expected in the coming years when user will experience much more user friendliness & betterment in Twitter.

Dorsey's aim is to transform any mobile device into a credit card reader which can accept credit cards and process transactions in less than 10 seconds. His vision is to make payment systems more accessible to anyone, anywhere and anytime.

Dorsey along with Biz Stone was awarded the Crunchie award for the best mobile startup in Oakland in 2000. MIT's Technology Review named him (in the Technology Review 35(TR35)) as an outstanding innovator under the age of 35.

Guy Kawasaki, Apple Evangelist

Guy Kawasaki is a former Apple evangelist and the Co-founder of Alltop. com. He is also considered as the Father of evangelism marketing. He is recognized as one of the first person to use the method of evangelism to promote a product brand through a blog. In the books written by Guy, *How to Drive Your Competition Crazy* and *The Art of the Start*, he has explained that every individual wants to makes their world a better place to live, and this is the biggest driving force behind evangelism marketing. His notion was Evangelist customers recruit new customers and spread their recommendations purely out of belief, not for the just receiving goods or money.

He was born on 30, August 1954, in Honolulu, Hawaii. His family was located in Kalihi Valley, a tough part of Honolulu. He was not from a very rich and affluent family, but his parents made great sacrifices for him and his sister, to provide them with all the luxuries of life. His father was a real estate broker, government official, state senator and a fireman in his long and distinguished career, while his mother was a home-maker.

He received his education from the Iolani School, from where he graduated in the year 1972. After that in 1976 he did his major in Psychology from Stanford. After that he went for law school at U.C. Davis, because his parents wanted him to be some professional like doctor or lawyer, but then he came to know that it was not his cup of tea and called a quit from the law school. After a year, he joined the MBA program at UCLA. While he was studying there, he joined Nova Stylings, a fine jewelry manufacturer. From there he learnt the skill of selling which he possessed his entire career. He is even an honorary doctorate from Babson College.

Guy worked at Nova for a few years and then he moved on to EduWare Services, which was an educational software company. EduWare was acquired by Peachtree Software and the company wanted Kawasaki to shift base to Atlanta. He left the job as he didn't like the place so much. He was on a look out for a good job when one of his friends from Stanford, called Mike Boich, got him a job at Apple in the year 1984. And then, there was no looking back for him. For four years he worked as an evangelist of Macintosh to different software and hardware developers.

In 1987, Guy left Apple, as his job as an evangelist was done. Then he started ACIUS, a Macintosh database company, as it had plenty of software by then. There they published a database called 4th Dimension. Till date it remains a great product manufactured by ACIUS. He ran the company for nearly two years and then he left the job to pursue his desire for writing books. He wrote as many as ten books and he is still a well known blogger. He has already written for Macworld, Forbes and Macuser.

In the year 1989, Kawasaki along with three of the World's best co-founders Kathryn Henkens, Jud Spencer and Will Mayall started another software company named Fog City Software. There they created software called Emailer, which was basically an email product. He sold the product to Claris and after that a list server product known as LetterRip.

In the year 1995, Kawasaki again joined Apple as an Apple fellow. His job after returning back to the institution was to rejuvenate and maintain the Macintosh cult, because at that time, the pundits of the IT industry perceived that Apple is going to die. Therefore, his duty was to revive the lost connections and maintain the association with the clients, which he was really good at. He worked there for a couple of years and again left Apple, once his job was done.

After leaving Apple for the second time, he started Garage.com, an angel investor matchmaking service, located in Silicon Valley, California, along with Rich Karlgaard of Forbes and Craig Johnson of Venture Law Group. They started the company together and went through a long distance before they developed a higher version of the website i.e. Garage.com, 2.0, which was created as an investment bank for assisting entrepreneurs to raise money from the venture capitalists. Now, Garage.com has another upper version 3.0, it is a venture capital firm called Garage Technology

Ventures, which makes direct investments for helping early stage technology companies.

He is currently working at Garage Technology Ventures as a Managing Director, and is also involved with RSS aggregator Alltop and rumor reporting site called Truemors. He is also the co-founder of Nononina, which is the company which created Alltop and Truemors website. He even works as an advisor for *jajah* and working with the Founder and CEO of *Visible Measures,* Brian Shin.

Though he has a been successful in almost every investment he has done, but one of the investment mistakes he did was, saying no to Yahoo! Guy was offered to be the C.E.O. of Yahoo! by one of Yahoo's original investors, Michael Moritz, a venture capitalist of Sequoia Capital. But then in late 1990s, Yahoo! was a tiny startup company and he was a bit skeptical about it. He was unsure of the business model of the company and couldn't see the way in which the company would generate revenue. Therefore, he declined the offer of investing in the company. He still considers it to be one of the biggest and the most expensive mistakes of his life.

He is also recognized as a well known blogger and author of ten books namely, *Rules for Revolutionaries* (2000), *Enchantment: The Art of Changing Hearts, Minds, and Actions* (2011), *How to Drive Your Competition Crazy* (1995), *Reality Check* (2008), *Selling the Dream* (1992), *The Art of the Start* (2004), *The Macintosh Way* (1990), *Database 101* (1991), *Hindsights* (1995) and *The Computer Curmudgeon* (1993). As a blogger, he writes the popular blog *How to Change the World.*

Kawasaki is an avid hockey fan and even plays hockey in Redwood City, Calif. When he was in high school, he was a linebacker of his football team.

Kawasaki is married to Beth. They worked together in Apple, where he first met her, and later on they tied the knot. They stay at San Francisco Bay Area with his wife and four children.

Evan Williams, Founder of Blogger.com

The best gift given by the almighty to a human being is to convey the feelings, emotions, and thoughts not only by expressions and by speaking the language, but also through a quiet and an impressive write-up which can enable the people to know you in a better way. Writing is an effective tool which thinkers and scholars use, to write about the betterment of the society. People know them and they get all the accolades for their writing work. Now, we need to think if this practice is good where only some selected intellectuals could get the highest opportunities to write on contemporary issues.

It was indeed a great thought process when Blogger was being developed by Evan Williams in 1999. During that phase, the Internet era had started. At that time, Blogger along with quite a few other internet applications came into the fore. Some of those applications were greeted warmly, but some could not sustain for long. Blogger too had its destiny and it was not a great success initially, but with time as the people understood the impact of writing and expressing their views independently, it started gaining popularity. Blogger was the first application which enabled the common people to express themselves and reach out a large number of readers. It also enabled readers to read material written on variety of topics. Blogger helped people to gain knowledge through reading. There is a saying that the more you read, the more you learn. People started their individual blogs, and as it gained the followers, fate of the Blogger also changed. Being in touch by following each other's views and thoughts was never as easy as Blogger actually made it, but we actually realize its importance now after more than a decade of the invention, and all thanks to Evan Williams, the founder of the site.

Evan Williams was born on March 31, 1972. He spent his early life in Clarks, Nebraska. He also pursued his studies at the University of Nebraska. Evan Williams is an American Entrepreneur known for his two top websites he has developed which are Blogger, developed by Pyra Labs and owned by him, and the another one is Twitter on which he worked as a CEO. He left the University of Nebraska only after one and a half years to make a career and he then worked in various organizations which provided him good technological experience such as in Key West, Dallas and Austin, Texas. His family had farms in Nebraska and he spent a bit of his time working there in farms. He was till then not established as anything he wanted to be, and was looking for an opportunity which he got in 1996 when he went to Sebastopol, California in Sonoma County where he started working for O'Reilly Media which was a technology publishing company. He was appointed in marketing department there, but that was not end of the world for him. His ability and technical knowledge later enabled him to work as an independent computer code writer. Computer code writing also brought him the opportunities to work with Intel and Hewlett-Packard at his doorstep. He learned and developed his technological innovations in San Francisco after he moved from Nebraska. Though making of Blogger was not the purpose he and his team were working for. We may call it an accident or a good fortune for Evan Williams.

The project they were working on was not going the way they wanted it to go. Then Blogger was created as a communication tool among the developers in his team to keep everyone aware of the happenings regarding the project, but Evan's insights brought him to a conclusion that this should be their project instead of one they are working on and are not getting much success. There were jokes used to go around in the lab regarding Blogger as how it should be their project now. That way Blogger was born, but no one knew a thing about it then as how it would work. It was Evan William's philosophy that ideas come accidentally, you cannot force them to come and create something you do not know, but still hoping for. The other ideology from Williams was that people believe what they see and you can only explain what you know.

Evan Williams calls his projects accidental successes, first one was Blogger and second one is Twitter and now he also owns a company named

Obvious. At the time when Blogger came into existence, people did not see it as a possible revolutionary product, but in 2003 Google owned it, and since then, Blogger is an essential part of internet fraternity.

Before Blogger was handed over to Google, it was Pyra Labs that used to develop management software, that are owned by Blogger. Evan Williams and Meg Hourihan were the founders of the Pyra Labs. Blogger was the first blogging application at that time and it had a big role in popularizing the term "blog." When financial crisis arose in the company, Pyra Labs' employee even worked without salary, but after some time many employees left the company as well as the co-founder Meg Hourihan. Lab did not have much income sources because Blogger at that time was not an earning tool for them. They lacked advertisements support as well. The lab was revived when Google eventually took control of it in 2003 and only after that, Blogger could become a popular product what it is now. The next year, in 2004, Evan Williams was awarded by PC Magazine as "People of the Year" in combination with Hourihan and Paul Bausch for their contribution in success of Blogger.

Blogger went through a moderation in design on May 9, 2004, and some of the features such as web standards, templates, and individual archive pages were added. Furthermore on August 14, 2006, Google launched the new beta version of Blogger which was titled with a code name "Invader." Through this version, users moved to the Google servers where some more features were welcoming them, such as use of different languages for blogging like German, Spanish, Italian, and French. The new version of Blogger was no more a beta version by December 2006 and Blogger's process was completely transferred to Google servers in May 2007. In 2007, regarding the number of unique visitors it got, Blogger was ranked at 16 in a list of 50 top websites.

Blogger has also become an element of Google toolbar now. Users can directly post links to their Blogger accounts using Google tool bar. "Blogger for Word" is another feature of Google which allows users to add word documents onto their blogs. Through this feature, blog posts can be edited even when user is offline. Other than that, Google derived AdSense is an extremely useful way to earn through a blog by advertising stuff. Blogger has been used as a tool through which people could speak their mind and make others know about contemporary issues. This is the reason that time to time Blogger has been blocked in some countries which had issues with the use of Blogger. Blogger has been banned in countries like Fiji, China, Iran, Pakistan, Syria, Arab Republic, Myanmar, Kazakhstan, Cuba, Turkey, and France at different periods of times.

When Blogger was acquired by Google, Williams too joined Google in Silicon Valley, but he could not adjust to their methodology at Google. Google's bureaucratic approach was not creating the best environment needed to imply innovative ideas in which Evan Williams believed. As a result, his coalition with Google could not stretch for a long time, and in October 2004, he left Google, as it was his destiny, to achieve some new milestones. Then he co-founded a podcast company called Odeo which was later, in April 2007, acquired by Sonic Mountain, but in between, he also established his Obvious Corp with his partner Biz Stone in late 2006.

Twitter was one of the projects that came out from Obvious Corp. Twitter is a social networking and micro-blogging website which changed the way of blogging by minimizing it to 140 characters per message line at once. These little message lines are now called tweets. In April 2007, Twitter turned into a new company in itself where Evan Williams was a co-founder, board member, and as well as an investor. Williams replaced Jack Dorsey as the CEO of Twitter in October 2008 while Jack Dorsey took over the position of chairman. Actually, Twitter's idea came out in a day long brain storming session of board of directors of Odeo. The idea was originally derived by Jack Dorsey who talked about a service where people can talk to each other using an SMS service. Its original project code name was twitter. On March 21, 2006, the project of Twitter was started and it was initially used as an internal communication tool for Odeo employees. On July 15, 2006, the full version of Twitter was introduced.

Evan Williams along with Biz Stone, Jack Dorsey, and some other members of Odeo also found a new company "Obvious" and they bought all the shares and stakes of Odeo and Twitter. In April 2007, Twitter became a separate company out of Obvious Corp. Twitter's popularity had increased quite a bit till 2007 and in South by Southwest festival, daily tweets were increased from 20,000 to 60,000. This festival earmarked the new era of online communication in the form of Twitter and it received highly positive opinions. Twitter saw a high percentage of increase in tweet numbers per quarter year which were 400,000 in 2007, went up to 100 million tweets in 2008, and by February 2010, number of tweets roared up to 50 million per day. As the number of Tweets per day went up, the ranking of Twitter too went up from 22nd to 3rd by January 2010 among social networking sites.

Twitter got an unmatched success in a very short span of time. Twitter was ranked the third most used social networking service in February 2009 by Compete.com. They decided this rank of Twitter by the number of unique monthly visitors and monthly visits to the site and the numbers were 6 million and 55 million, respectively. It was an amazing feat considering Twitter was only 2 year old in the business. Twitter had 105,779,710 registered users till April 14, 2010, and 300,000 new users join Twitter every day and the number of unique visitors a month has increased to 180 million. Dick Costolo became the new CEO of twitter on October 4th, 2010, when Williams stepped down from the position. Company also launched new Twitter version in October 2010. Alexa's Web Traffic ranked Twitter one of the 10 most visited websites. Company's value in February 2011 was estimated at $3.7 billion.

In normal life, Evan Williams is a pure vegetarian and lives in the San Francisco Bay Area with his wife Sara Morishige. Philosophy of Evan Williams can be inspiring for others as how someone can learn from mistakes and accidents done at work and moderate them for success. His most of the successful projects have been started by accidental stumbling. They were never intended to be the way they actually turned out to be, but it was the vision in his eyes that he could see and think differently. Who would have known and understood the Blogger in 1999 other than him and advent of twitter just enlightened the fact even more.

Jimmy Donal Wales—Founder of Wikipedia

Every success is built on a concept; Wikipedia is a great example of it. When we want to gather any information about any topic we look for an encyclopedia, and if we are at the internet we have Wikipedia, single repository of human knowledge. And this revolutionary repository was created by Jimmy Donal Wales, an internet entrepreneur who gave the world a place to learn and share knowledge.

Word "Wiki" (Hawaiian word) means "quick". Wikipedia is collection of articles and information related to each and every field we can think of, collectively written by volunteers who wanted to share information. Jimmy Wales provided that platform to share the information which makes Wikipedia so unique in nature. Motto behind this initiative is information for all in the world. Jimmy Wales said "My original concept was to provide a free encyclopedia for every single person in the world"

Talking of Jimmy Donal Wales, this visionary man was born in Huntsville, Alabama (United States of America), on August 7 or 8, 1966. He comes from a middle class family. His father managed a grocery store and his mother, Doris, and grandmother, Erma, ran a small school named House of Learning which was in the tradition of One Room School House. Jimmy Wales attended that school till 8ᵗʰ standard. Jimmy Credited the Montessori Method of the School Philosophy. Jimmy used to through the Britannica and World Book encyclopedias.

He graduated from the Randolph School, a university-preparatory school in Huntsville. He graduated at the age of sixteen. He admitted that studying there was expensive for his family but education being passion of his family kept him there. He received his bachelor's degree from the

Auburn University in Finance. Then he entered the Ph.D Program in Finance at University of Alabama, He received a master's degree from here, He then joined Ph.D Finance Program at Indiana University. But he lost interest before completing his dissertation & started his career in Finance as a research director in a Chicago based firm.

By the end of 1996 he changed course of his career by starting a dot com company called Bomis with his partner Tim Shell. Bomis was a search portal. Bomis started an open directory project search directory. These search related pages generated revenue from advertising and affiliate marketing. Bomis provided the revenue to create the online encyclopedia. Bomis hosted Nupedia in 2000, Nupedia was a reviewed free online encyclopedia written by experts. Lary Sanger was invited to be editor in chief for Nupedia. Since expert written and reviewed documents were time consuming so building an encyclopedia of this nature was much likely and time saving.

According to Wales, "The idea was to have thousands of volunteers writing articles for an online encyclopedia in all languages. Initially we found ourselves organizing the work in a very top-down, structured, academic, old-fashioned way. It was no fun for the volunteer writers because we had a lot of academic peer review committees who would criticize articles and give feedback. It was like handing in an essay at grad school, and basically intimidating to participate in". [5]

Therefore, in 2001 Jimmy Wales came up with this unique concept of Wikipedia (Quick Encyclopedia). This was a collaborated project which was open for editing for all users. Initially this concept was adapted in Nupedia, but this was not quite welcomed by the experts at Nupedia. Eventually it was launched as a separate web site, popularly known as Wikipedia.

At the beginning, experts and Jimmy himself was not very sure about the success of this project as articles posted would be amateurish and would

---

[5]   http://www.newscientist.com/article/mg19325896.300-interview-knowledge-to-the-people.html

lack in authenticity. But the response was overwhelming; article stated pouring in at a furious speed.

Encouraged by the response a small team of editors was set to fine tune these articles and work as a regulatory authority. Initially Sanger guided the project. But the idea of a free document with contributions from common man was Jimmy's. Sanger left the project in Feb 2002, Bomis stopped funding this project. Later this was developed as a nonprofit foundation.

There were several controversies which sparked due to the news of dispute between the co-founders of Wikipedia, namely, Jimmy Wales and Lary Sanger. Later on the assertion of Wales being the sole founder of the website, added fuel to the controversies. Although, later on Wales corrected himself and pronounced Sanger to be the co-founder of the website. His formal designation in Wikipedia foundation is of board member and chairman. But well known as constitutional monarch and spiritual leader of Wikipedia.

Describing his role in the organization Jimmy Wales said "to create and distribute a free encyclopedia of the highest possible quality to every single person on the planet in their own language,' that's who I am. That's what I am doing. That's my life goal." He also stated that, "I have always viewed the mission of Wikipedia to be much bigger than just creating a killer website. We're doing that of course, and having a lot of fun doing it, but a big part of what motivates us is our larger mission to affect the world in a positive way."

Diversifying the area of Wikipedia he founded Wikimedia foundation in 2003 whose purpose was to establish general policy for encyclopedia and other sister projects. Wales estimated that Wikipedia is worth US$3 billion, he believed donation has made this success. There are few controversies wrapped in his tenure in Wikimedia as he was accused of misusing foundation funds which Wales has denied. In 2004, Wales and fellow member in Wikimedia foundation Angela Beesley founded Wikia a for profit organization. It's a collection of different wikis like memory Alpha on Star Trek and wikiapedia on star wars. Wikia also offered an open source search engine. Wikia search intended to give competition to Google. But it did not succeed and was closed in 2009. Wales stepped down as Wikia CEO in 2009. Apart from these roles Wales is a public spokes person represented by the Harry Walker agency.

Jimmy Wales was inspired by the philosophy of "Objectivist to the core" developed by Ayn Rand in the novel "The Fountainhead". He described his political views as "Center-right". Jimmy Wales have refused to censor politically sensitive articles by China. Wales believed in freedom of information which led to suits by big companies like Google against Wikipedia. He also did not like WikiLeaks to use the word Wiki as they did not maintain the essence of Wiki which is collaborative editing. His way of promoting Wikipedia has been criticized as altruistic which he has rejected saying "Sacrificing your own value for others".

In personal life Jimmy Wales has been married twice, at first he was married at the age of 20 to Pam, she was co-worker at grocery store at Alabama. In the year 1997, he married Christine Rohan in Florida. She was working for Mitsubishi Steel. They have a daughter. After separation with second wife, Wales moved to San Diego. Later he shifted to Florida in 2002. He has been reportedly engaged to Kate Garvey, former diary secretary of Tony Blair.

Jimmy Wales has received numerous awards, most recent being Gottlieb Duttweiler Prize. Earlier he has been awarded the Monaco Media Prize, the 2009 Nokia foundation annual award, the Business Process Award at the 7th Annual Innovation Awards and summit by The Economist. The 2008 Global Brand Icon of the Year Award and on behalf of the Wikimedia project the Quadriga award of Werkstatt Deutschland for A Mission of Enlightenment.

Jimmy Wales Once said "Imagine a world in which every single person on the planet is given free access to the sum of all human knowledge. That's what we're doing." "His goal is to provide people a free encyclopedia to each person in the world, in their own language. Not just in a 'free beer' kind of way, but also in the free speech kind of way." This depicts the greatness of the person; he is truly one of the kings of internet.

Jerry Yang & David Filo, Co-Founders of Yahoo

David Filo

David Filo was born on April 20, 1966 at Wisconsin. He is well known as the co-founder of Yahoo, and an American businessman.

David Filo developed a server program for yahoo by using the C programming language which was server-side scripting software, which used to show variable Filo Server Pages when you visit to the Yahoo web site, but later Yahoo switched to PHP scripting.

Filo was born at Wisconsin, but at the age of 6 he was shifted to Moss Bluff, Louisiana, situated in a suburb of Lake Charles. Filo completed his graduation from Sam Houston High School and then pursued Computer Engineering from Tulane University, where he went through the Dean's Honor Scholarship. He also got a degree of MS from Stanford University.

In 2006, Filo was ranked 240th richest person in the world with $2.9 billion of worth. David Filo is also known as a philanthropist. He donates money for the good of human being. He donated $30 million to the Tulane University, so that they can work for the betterment of the School of Engineering. His wife Angela Buenning is a photographer and also works as a teacher.

Jerry Yang

Jerry Yang was born in Taipei, Taiwan, on November 6, 1968. At the age of 10, Yang moved to San Jose, California along with his mother and younger brother. Yang's father had died when he was only 2 years old. Though his mother was an English teacher in China, but according to him when he moved to US, he only knew one English word and he learnt English and became fluent within 3 years through an AP English Class.

Yang did his graduation from Sierramont Middle School and Piedmont Hills High School. After that, he pursued BS and MS degrees in electrical engineering from Stanford University. He was a member of Phi Kappa Psi fraternity at Stanford University. In 1994, when Yang was still studying Electrical Engineering at Stanford University, he developed an internet website "Jerry and Dave's Guide to the World Wide Web" in company with David Filo. The website consisted of a directory of other websites. The website was later renamed as Yahoo! and it became very popular among the users in no time.

They soon realized the importance of the website that they have created and understood how it can be a good business proposition and therefore, co-founded Yahoo! Inc. in April 1995. Yahoo was first launched in Santa Clara, California, with quarter in Sunnyvale, California, USA.

Yahoo! was initially started as a web portal which had a web directory to provide a range of products and services for online users. In all these years, since Yahoo! was launched, it had become a leading internet brand. It has successful partnership with several telecommunication services and attracts highest number of user traffic on its network which has helped increase its value and rank.

On November 17, 2008, The Wall Street Journal reported that Jerry Yang would be stepping down as the CEO as soon as they find a replacement. This change was due to the stagnant position of Yahoo in the stock market. Neither the stock prices of the company were increasing nor was it able to generate the amount of profit it was expected to. This led to extreme criticism by the investors as they were unsatisfied by the performance of the company and held Yang to be responsible for it. On January 13, 2009, almost about three months later, Silicon Valley professional Carol Bartz was appointed as the new CEO of Yahoo! Although Yang remained as the member of board of directors of Yahoo! and also designated as Chief Yahoo.

Yang's wife is Akiko Yamazaki is Japanese and was brought up Costa Rica. Akiko Yamazaki completed her graduation in industrial engineering stream from Stanford University. They first met each other in 1992 at the Stanford University for Kyoto overseas program. Along with Yahoo, Yang's professional life also includes a membership on the Board of Directors of Alibaba, the Asian Pacific Fund, Cisco, and as well as Yahoo! Japan. He also works as a trustee at the Stanford University.

Jerry Yang is also a philanthropist. He and his wife donated $75 million to Stanford University for their alma mater. A bulk of this money was spent in construction of the building block named after Jerry and his wife that is "Jerry Yang and Akiko Yamazaki Environment and Energy Building." The building was designed by Boora Architects of Portland, Oregon, and was constructed by Hathaway Dinwiddie Construction Company of San Francisco, California. The building also nicknamed as Y2E2. This building consists of multi-disciplinary research block, teaching block, and lab.

In an incident, Chinese Authorities criticized Jerry Yang for his statement regarding an arrest of a Chinese journalist, Shi Tao. It was an unfortunate step by the government of China when they ordered Chinese media to not cover the fifteenth anniversary of the Tiananmen Square Protests on June 4, 1989. At that time, Chinese journalist Shi too used yahoo to send a mail to a site in support of democracy and Yahoo! had provided the IP addresses of the senders, the recipients, and the time of the message to Chinese security agencies. As the consequence, Shi Tao was later convicted for "divulging state secrets abroad." Jerry Yang was criticized for these internationally.

Later Yang clarified that he just worked according to the rules of the country as they were doing business in China and they had to cooperate with the government authorities due to the laws. But as Yahoo is a US company, it was a controversial statement by Yang and according to some critics, it violated international law and US Congress had passed a law in 1989 according to which they had prevented US online companies from providing any "crime control and detection" equipment or software or information to the Chinese Government. The New York Times also published news that a civil suit was filed against Yahoo by political prisoner

Wang Xiaoning and other journalists. They accused yahoo to help the Chinese government against the journalists, as an outcome of which Shi Tao and other journalists had to undergo the torture and imprisonment by the government authorities.

Later Jerry Yang was given a notice by the US Government to explain about his comment on the incident and Yahoo's role in the arrests of Shi Tao and other journalists, in October 2007. On November 14, 2007, Yahoo paid undisclosed compensation to the affected families and settled the issues. Jerry Yang met the families and explained that what he did was right for everyone. Democratic Congressman, Tom Lantos, the chairman of the United States House Committee on Foreign Affairs responded in a harsh way to Jerry and criticized Yahoo to take so much time before helping the families of affected journalists who were forced to go to jail because of their foolishness.

Jerry Yang accepted these allegations and felt sorry for the journalist and their families. He was upset with all the happenings and he decided to talk to Condoleezza Rice, Secretary of State, and requested her to try and free the dissidents from jail. Other than that, he also started a fund named Yahoo! Human Rights Fund to provide "humanitarian and legal support" in these kinds of cases. The first thing they did by using that fund is organizing and financing the Laogai Museum. The museum was opened by a Chinese dissident Harry Wu who showcased China's Laogai penal system there.

Though all these good works did not yield good result in favor of Yang and the consequences of the arrest of Li Zhi through the help of Yahoo were coming continuously as another lawsuit was filed against Yahoo! on behalf of Zheng Cunzhu and Guo Quan. They both blamed Yahoo for their property and business loss. Complaint was filed along the lines of violation of international laws and unfair business practices by Yahoo, and for false imprisonment and assault.

In May 2008, Microsoft offered Jerry Yang and the board of directors $33 per share to take over whole of Yahoo! for a total sum of USD44.6 billion, but Yahoo! refused it and for that, Yang was criticized by the shareholders as it was a lucrative offer. Yahoo! wanted a bigger offer and said this offer is undervaluing them, but Microsoft canceled the deal and left the road for others and decided against the takeover. In the end, it proved to be a big loss for shareholders as Yahoo's shares were valued at $14 in November 2008. Google in company of Yahoo was trying to start commercial search advertising, but they did not go ahead as they had suspicions of its adverse effects in the market.

In an interesting turn of events, Yahoo! and Microsoft again came together to tackle Google and on July 29, 2009, they announced a search deal and in the process Microsoft launched its own search engine called Bing.

Yahoo's revenue model mostly depends on marketing and advertising. In 2009, almost 88% of the revenue was earned through marketing. Yahoo search engine plays a huge role in achieving the revenue target as advertisers publish their ads on Yahoo search results and Yahoo is paid for every search by the advertisers. Till January, 2010, Yahoo had the largest online display advertising share in the world. According to JP Morgan, Yahoo had the 17% of market share for display ads in US market while number two was Microsoft and they had 11%, of share, and AOL was lagging behind at 7% with number three position.

Yahoo portal publishes contents like latest news, entertainment, and sports. Other Yahoo! services like Yahoo mail, Yahoo maps, Yahoo finance, Yahoo groups, and Yahoo Messenger can also be accessed through the portal. Other than these services, there are several Yahoo brands that are popular among the users such as Yahoo mobile, Yahoo meme, Yahoo music, Yahoo, movies, Yahoo real estate, Yahoo travel, Yahoo shopping, Yahoo widgets, and Yahoo web analytical, etc. Yahoo earns revenues through these services as well. In addition to these services, Yahoo also has some non-Yahoo branded sites and services which include Fire Eagle, Flickr, FoxyTunes, Upcoming, and Wretch.

Yahoo is an international portal and an online service and is available in more than 20 portals. World.yahoo.com is an official directory of all the international Yahoo websites and all these international sites are mostly owned by Yahoo with two exceptions, one of Japan, where they have

34.9% of minority stakes and second one is in Australia where they share 50-50% partnership with Seven Network.

Yahoo also had joint venture agreements with SoftBank in some of the European country sites such as Germany, UK, and France as well as in Asian countries Korea and Japan which they bought back from SoftBank in November 2005. Yahoo also started Romanian version of Yahoo on March 8, 2011, which was getting postponed since 2008 for some reasons. According to The New York Times, Yahoo has the biggest database of their users. On May 22, 2008, there was an article published which revealed that Yahoo has 2 petabytes of database warehouse which helps Yahoo to analyze the state of mind of users and their behaviors. Yahoo can collect a large amount of data in comparison to other online services through Yahoo website.

According to Yahoo, this is the largest database that existed in the world at that time and they were expecting it to grow up to 10 petabytes till 2009. Internet communication services of Yahoo such as Yahoo! Messenger and Yahoo! Mail are one of the two most popular services among internet users and Yahoo Mail provides unlimited storage facility since March 2007 when Yahoo first announced it. My Web, Yahoo! Personals, Yahoo! 360°, Delicious, Flickr, and Yahoo! Buzz are social networking services which consist of user-generated content. There was news about Yahoo closing services like Yahoo! Buzz, MyBlogLog, Delicious, and some other services that came out in December 2010. September 20, 2007, Yahoo! Photos was closed for Flickr. On October 16, 2007, Yahoo also stopped providing any bug fixing solution on Yahoo! 360° as they were going to start another universal profile service and abandoned it in early 2008.

Yahoo also owns 40% shares of Alibaba Group, which is an online selling and buying service. They initially used to have the sales of shark-made product on their sites and for that they were highly criticized and that was a subject of controversy then, but later, they banned showing these kinds of products on all of their shopping platforms on January 1, 2009. Yahoo announced to purchase 40% shares of Alibaba group on August 10, 2005. Alibaba Group's original founder is Jack Ma who still stayed in charge of the group. Alibaba is now spread up to 70 cities regions that include UK, USA, Japan, China, Korea, India, and Hong Kong, and with

22,000 employees working under the shadow, Alibaba group in itself is a huge online service. In one dramatic episode, when Yahoo and adobe became targets of hackers and were facing heaps of cyber attacks on their network, then Google threatened to quit China in an announcement on January 12, 2010.

Eric Schmidt, CEO of Google

It will be always a dream for many of world's top management gurus today to lead a company like Google. Eric Schmidt, CEO of Google managed the company since 2001 and took it to its zenith alongside the duo co-founders Larry Page and Sergey Brin.

Eric Schmidt the computer whizkid was born on 27th April 1955 in Washington, D.C. He grew up in Blacksburg, Virginia and completed his graduation from Yorktown High school. After earning a BSEE degree from Princeton University in 1976, he acquired an MS in 1979 for designing and implementing a network linking from the University of California. In 1982 he earned a PhD in EECS with a dissertation about the problems of managing distributed software development and tools for solving these problems. As a part-time professor he also taught at Stanford B-School. He was joint author of "a lexical analyzer and an important tool for compiler construction".

In various IT companies, including Bell Labs, Zilog and Xerox's famed Palo Alto Research Center (PARC), Schmidt held a series of technical positions early in his career. In 1983 he joined Sun Microsystems and later became the President of Sun Technology Enterprises. In 1997, he was appointed CEO and chairman of the board of Novell. But after the acquirement of Cambridge Technology Partners he left Novell.

In 2001 Google founders Larry Page and Serge Brin recruited Schmidt to run their company under the guidance of venture capitalists John Doerr and Michael Moritz. In March 2001 Schmidt joined Google's board of directors as chairman and in August 2001 he became CEO of Google. Schmidt shares responsibility for Google's daily operations with founders Page and Brin at Google and these three run Google as a triumvirate.

Schmidt possesses the legal responsibilities as a typical CEO of a public company. He also manages the vice presidents and the sales organization. Google's website displays that Schmidt also focuses on "building the corporate infrastructure needed to maintain Google's rapid growth as a company and on ensuring that quality remains high while product development cycle times are kept to a minimum."[6] During his tenure at Google he has given steady growth while expanding Google's reach. He has also introduced new products from the popular web based email service Gmail in Germany & UK. In 2007, Schmidt ranked first on the list of PC World's 50 most important people on the web, along with Google co-Founders Larry Page and Sergey Brin.

In 2009 an advisory agency Brendan Wood International considered Schmidt as one of the "TopGun CEOs". During his term Google rose from popular search Engine to a dominant player in online video and mobile devices and is now stretching out to computers and internet TV. Core technologies became Google's search engine. Their combined efforts have vastly enhanced internet use, enabling people to find information and navigate the World Wide Web with great ease, speed and effectiveness. On January 20, 2011 Schmidt stepped down as CEO of Google, but he continues as the executive chairman of the company and acts as an adviser to co-founders Page and Brin. But later Page replaced Schmidt as CEO on April 4, 2011.

The 2011 book "How Google Thinks, Works, and Shapes Our Lives" by Steven Levy states that in 2001, Schmidt requested the wrong information that 'he has made political donation' be removed from Google search results. The request was not fulfilled. But Schmidt has denied the ever occurrence of this incident. On August 28, 2006 Schmidt was elected as one of the board of directors to Apple. On August 3, 2009, it was announced that Schmidt would resign from the board of directors at Apple due to conflict of interests amid the growing competition between Google and Apple. Schmidt "was a campaign advisor and major donor to Barack Obama, and when he announced he was leaving that perch, he planned to remain 'at the forefront of Google's government relations team.' And Obama even has considered him for Commerce Secretary."

---

[6]   http://www.google.com/about/corporate/company/execs.html#eric

Being an informal advisor to the Obama presidential campaign Schmidt began campaigning from October 19, 2008, on behalf of the candidate. He had been elected for the position of chief technology officer which Obama created in his administration. In announcing his endorsement for Obama, Schmidt jokingly said that with his $1.00 salary, he would be getting a tax cut. After Obama won the election, Schmidt was a member of transition advisory board of President Obama. He proposed that the easiest way to solve all of the problems of the United States at once, at least in the domestic policy, is by a stimulus program that rewards renewable energy and, over time and attempts to replace fossil fuels with renewable energy. Since, he has become a new member of the President's Council of Advisors on Science and Technology PCAST.

Schmidt lives with his wife Wendy in Atherton, California. His name is also mentioned in the list of ARTnews 200 top art collectors. Eric Schmidt and his wife Wendy were working with a San Francisco architectural firm, Heart Howerton. The firm specializes in large-scale land use. On the island of Nantucket, Eric and Wendy have inaugurated several projects. The purpose of these projects is to sustain the unique character of the island and to minimize the impact of seasonal visitation on the island's core community. Wendy Schmidt declared an award of the Wendy Schmidt Oil Cleanup X CHALLENGE. This is a challenge award for efficient capturing of crude oil from seawater motivated by the Deepwater Horizon oil spill.

STEVE CASE, CO-FOUNDER OF AOL

Stephen McConnell Case, aka "Steve" was born on August 21, 1958, at Honolulu, Hawaii, United States. He is an American businessman, but well known as the Chairman, Chief Executive Officer and Co-founder of American Online (AOL). Steve's father was an attorney, while his mother was a school teacher. He is the third child amongst his four siblings. From a very early age he showed signs of being a businessman. When he was just six years of age, he used to help his bother Daniel at a juice stall. He along with his brothers sold seeds and magazine subscriptions. They started Case Enterprises, a mail order company.

In 1976, Case graduated from Punahou School and then he attended the Central Union Church. In the year 1980, Case graduated from Williams College in Williamstown, Massachusetts, with a degree in political science. After completing his graduation he worked at Procter & Gamble in Cincinnati, Ohio, as an assistant brand manager, for the next two years. In the year 1982, he managed pizza development at Pizza Hut Inc. in Wichita, Kansas.

At a Consumer Electronics show in Las Vegas, Case was introduced to the CEO of Control Video Corporation, Bill von Meister, by his older brother Daniel, who was an investment banker in January 1983. At that time Control Video was still a struggling company. They offered him the post of a marketing assistant and he wasted no time and accepted the offer with open arms, as by then he was very much interested and wanted to be a part of the interactive world of computer based entertainment and communication.

Control Video was Washington-based Company and was mainly engaged in providing online gaming features and services to Atari computer owners. But as Atari Computers faltered, the gaming service lost its demand and

Control Video lost their major client. Therefore, they had to cut on the number of staffs to much extent and Case became the company's marketing director. Their new CEO was James Kimsey, when the company signed a deal with Commodore Computers to manage their online gaming service. In 1985, the company was renamed as Quantum Computer Services.

In 1987, after tirelessly hunting for new investors Case landed up to a deal with Apple Computers to provide them with custom online services. He also signed a similar deal with Tandy, but in 1989 when Apple withdrew its contract, both the company as well as Case, again drew into a situation of crisis. At that point of time, Case came up with the solution of creating its own branded online service. He thought of such online service which is independent of any hardware manufacturer, and he named the service as American Online.

In the year 1989, American Online or AOL made its nationwide debut. Quantum Computer Services was changed to America Online, Inc. in 1991, as a subscription based online community. During its early days of commencement, AOL had direct competition with Prodigy, Genie and CompuServe, which were all backed by the big names of the industry like Sears, General Electric and IBM. But unlike others, AOL was easy to use, with user friendly and well designed environment, which allowed average tech savvy consumers to work with ease and attracted a huge number of them who were hesitant to frightening high-tech aura of the superior text based corporate services.

AOL was expanding very quickly. By the second half of 1994, American Online acquired more than a million subscribers and already gave a start in expanding overseas. CompuServe was threatened by the increasing number of AOL subscribers; therefore they tried to acquire the company for $50 million. At that time it was quite a considerable amount and many observers had the opinion that American Online is doing a mistake turning the offer down. AOL went public in the year 1992, at that time it was still behind CompuServe in its subscriber base, but within three years time, AOL surpassed CompuServe to become the number one online service provider.

In 1991, Kimsey declared Case to be his successor. He was grooming Case from the beginning to lead the company. Gradually, Case took over American Online's everyday operations, and from a marketing executive he became the CEO of the company in the year 1993, while Kimsey remained as the Chairman of AOL. In the year 1997, Steve took over the complete duty of being a Chairman as well as the CEO after the retirement of Kimsey.

AOL came to the fore front as the primary provider of the online content, but as more and more people gained access over internet through their telephone services, AOL's reign seemed to come to an end. Feeling the change in the internet atmosphere Case reacted quickly and adapted the services in such a manner that it can reach to most of the average populace of the country, making it the most popular and accepted portal for the general consumer to enter the web world. AOL soon reassured its position as the top most Internet service provider, due to its easy, user friendly interface.

Even Microsoft couldn't dominate the web world with its lead in system software. More than once they tried to acquire or neutralize the control of AOL, however Case was stern to his words, and in due time both telecommunications giant AT&T and Microsoft came forward for partnership agreements with AOL. AOL acquired the online service of its old competitor CompuServe, in the year 1998, and just one year later, the maker of very well accepted Internet browsing software, Netscape Communications, in 1999. Time and again, with his achievements and intelligence, Case has proved his critics wrong. While they professed demise of the company, Case created AOL, as the first blue chip company of the Internet and created history.

Under the leadership of Case, AOL guided the internet industry in such areas as integrating software technology into schools, consumer privacy as well as ensuring the protection of children in the virtual world. Case was successful in making the Internet as a part of the American house just like television or telephone. He, in no time, identified the subsequently challenges of getting broadband access for the users, and incorporating the earlier media world of the music and the film industries with the latest media world of the Internet and computers.

"The deal of the century" was cracked by Case in the year 2001, when he devised a big merger acquiring Time Warner, the entertainment and multimedia giant for $164 billion in cash and stock. Case served the pooled enterprise, AOL Time Warner as the Chairman, for nearly two years. AOL Time Warner was then the largest media enterprise in the world. As the Chairman of AOL Time Warner, Case supervised an exceptional set of media holdings, which included the Warner Brothers film studio, Turner Broadcasting, Time Inc. publishing and CNN.

In the year 2002, AOL's membership reached the summit of 27 million, but the expected joint venture among old and new media enterprises never materialized, and the company witnessed an industry-wide slump for Internet providers. This was quite shocking for AOL, whose losses became a severe burden for the parent company. Eventually, in the year 2003, the parent enterprise dropped AOL from the name of the company. From the post of Chairman, Steve Case relegated as Chairman of the Board of Directors and subsequently in October 2005, he left the board altogether.

Amongst several initiatives taken by Case in the initial years of AOL, he himself championed many pioneering online interactive games and titles, which includes graphical chat environments Habitat in 1986 and Club Caribe in 1989. In the year 1988, he championed the first online interactive fiction game series QuantumLink Serial by Tracy Reed, Quantum Space, the first completely automated Play by email game in 1989, plus the title Neverwinter Nights of the original Dungeons & Dragons, the first Massively Multiplayer Online Role Playing Game (MMORPG) in 1991, to portray the adventure with graphics rather than text.

In the year 2005, Case wrote down in The Washington Post that "It's now my view that it would be best to 'undo' the merger by splitting Time Warner into several independent companies and allowing AOL to set off on its own path." [7]

---

[7] http://www.seattlepi.com/default/article/AOL-founder-calls-for-breakup-of-Time-Warner-1189722.php

In 1997, Case along with his wife Jean Case created a company which they named as Case Foundation. He is the Chairman of the Case Foundation. In April, 2005, he founded Revolution LLC, an investment firm, which is a parent company to several other companies. He is the Chairman of Accelerate Brain Cancer Cure (ABC2), a non-profit enterprise for funding brain cancer research, which he founded along with his late brother Dan, in the year 2001. Case has also served as the Vice-chairman of the Committee to Encourage Corporate Philanthropy and served Business Strengthening America as the founding organizer. Along with this, Case is a chief investor of two Hawaiian businesses—Maui Land & Pineapple and Grove Farm of Kauai.

In 2009, Case was introduced in the Junior Achievement U.S. Business Hall of Fame; he was selected as the Citizen Regent of the Smithsonian Institution in 2011. Case was furthermore honored with the National Mentoring Partnership Leadership Award.

He is even serving as the Co-chairman of the Democracy Project at the Bipartisan Policy Center. Since more than 20 years his residence is at Washington, D.C. but he still remains close and actively involved to his hometown Hawaii and invests in new enterprise that offers new working models for agriculture as well as sustainable development in the state. He also donated $10 million to Punahou School, from where he did his elementary schooling. He donated the fund for building a junior high school, which would be named after his parents.

In the subsequent years, it was widely accepted that the merger between Time Warner and AOL had completely failed, which compelled the joint venture to write off the agreement paying $100 billion in charges, in 2009. The parent company announced that they are spinning off AOL as an independent enterprise.

The collapse of the AOL—Time Warner fusion is the focus of a book written in 2005, by Nina Munk titled, *Fools Rush In: Steve Case, Jerry Levin, and the Unmaking of AOL Time Warner*, along with a photograph on the cover of Time Warner's Jerry Levin and Case embracing each other at the declaration of the joint venture.

Case's father, Daniel H. Case, serves Case Lombardi & Pettit, a Hawaiian law firm, as the founding partner. While Carol, his mother, is a school teacher. His siblings are Carin, Dan and Jeff. In June 2002, his brother Dan died at an age of 44 from brain cancer.

Case tied the knot with Joanne Barker, in 1985. He met Joanne while he was attending William College. They had three children. In 1996, they divorced each other, and after two years, in 1998, he married Jean Villanueva, former AOL executive. Their marriage ceremony was officiated by Billy Graham. Case resides in a mansion that was the childhood home of Jacqueline Bouvier at McLean, Virginia, with his wide, four daughters and a son.

Pierre Omidyar, Founder of eBay

One of the most popular online auction website, eBay, was founded by Pierre Morad Omidyar, who was born in Paris, France on June 21, 1967. Omidyar is an Iranian-American entrepreneur. He is also known for his philanthropic activities and is also a known economist. He and his wife Pam both largely believe in philanthropy and for that, in 2004, they established Omidyar Network to work in non-profitable sectors. He also serves as a chairman of eBay.

His parents were emigrated from Iran to France before he was born. His parents were sent there by his grandparents to study in university. Elahe Mir-Djalali Omidyar, his mother, studied linguistic and completed her doctorate at Sorbonne. She later worked as an academic person. His father was a surgeon. When he was 6 years of age, his family shifted to USA and there he lived most of his life in Washington, D.C.

He studied in Potomac School where he started taking interest in computers, especially as he reached 9th grade. He then went to St. Andrew's Episcopal School located in Potomac, Maryland. In 1984, he passed from St. Andrew's. Thereafter, he completed his graduation in computer science in 1988 from Tufts University. After that, he was hired by an Apple subsidiary called Claris and worked on developing MacDraw. Pierre co-founded Ink Development in 1991 which was a pen-based computing company. The company was later renamed as eShop and was re-branded as an e-commerce venture.

Actually, the most popular auction site eBay came to life as a result of Omidyar's weekend holidays, when he wrote the coding of the site at the age of 28 which became one of the super internet brands in no time. On Monday, September 4, 1995, it was Labor Day when the site was launched with name "Auction Web." He hosted this website on a site he had developed to put information about "Ebola" virus. His first choice for the name of this was "echobay," but he was informed by the hosting service that the domain name is already registered.

After that he manipulated the name by cutting "cho" and derived a new name "eBay." It was a quick and on the spot decision by Omidyar to change the name because of unavailability of his desired name and he also did not wanted to visit Sacramento again for this purpose. According to some reports, Omidyar started eBay to promote his wife's candy. A public relation manager of the company had disclosed this story to interest the media in 1997 and came out in 2002 in a book written by Adam Cohen which eBay officials later confirmed. Services of eBay were free at the start of the website, but later on to make up the cost of internet service provider, they implied charges for their services.

In 1996, Jeffrey Skoll joined eBay and Meg Whitman was appointed as President and CEO of the company in March 1998. Meg retired from her position in 2008 after doing a great job for the company. Company introduced a public offer in September 1998, which went highly successful. Omidyar had 178 million shares which were estimated at $4.45 billion by July 2008. Omidyar had also done some investments at Montage Resort & Spa located in Laguna Beach, California.

Omidyar started "Civil Beat" in Honolulu, which is an online news service, in 2010 to cover civil affairs in Hawaii.

For philanthropic purposes, Omidyar established Omidyar Network which works as an investment firm made to work on controlling markets and provide us the power of market to make life of the people better. The network was established in 2004 by Pierre Omidyar and Pam, his wife. Omidyar Network invests in different organizations which work in economic, social, and political sectors to instill innovations and changes in the society for the betterment of the people. These are mostly non-profit organizations. Omidyar Network has supported many profit and non-profit organizations and has invested $270 million by now. Network encourages new developments in microfinance, property rights, government transparency, and social media.

Pierre was declared 145th richest person in the world by Forbes in March 2011. He is also known as the richest person of Iranian descent.

The biggest reason for this wealth of Pierre is eBay Inc. which is an "Internet Consumer-To-Consumer Corporation." One of most popular online shopping and suction website eBay.com is managed by eBay Inc. This website provides facility to buy and sell various kinds of products and services all over the world. eBay was founded by Pierre Omidyar in 1995. eBay is one website which did not go down even in dot-com bubble which had finished many webs ventures in its storm. In the last 15 years, eBay.com has become billion dollar business while running its services in more than 30 countries. eBay had started operating in a "set-time" auction format but later also converted to "Buy It Now" shopping. Shopping can be done by online money transfers like PayPal, online event ticket trading like StubHub, UPC, online classified advertisements like Kijiji or eBay Classifieds, ISBN, or SKU such as Half.com.

AuctionWeb, this was the actual name with which eBay was started in its early days by French-born Iranian computer programmer Pierre Omidyar in San Jose, California, on September 3, 1995. The site was a part of his personal website which was consisted of Omidyar's expressions on Ebola virus. It is reported that broken laser pointer was the first item that was old through eBay for $14.83. There was an incident regarding this purchase which amazed Omidyar and made him think about it.

He asked the person who auctioned that, if he understood that the laser pointer was broken. He was replied back and buyer explained, "I'm a collector of broken laser pointers." There was another story regarding the start of eBay which has been circulated regularly that he started eBay to trade Pez candy dispensers by his fiancée, though in 2002 in a book, it was reported that this story was just spread to interest the media by a media manager of eBay which was later confirmed by the management.

The first employee of was Chris Agarpao while and Jeffrey Skoll was appointed as first president in early 1996. The company made their entry in third-party licensing deal in November 1996 with a company named Electronic Travel Auction and started using their SmartMarket Technology through which they sold plane tickets and other travel products.

Site was progressing rapidly by each passing day and while in 2006, they had total of 250,000 auction is a whole year, in January 1997, they achieved 2,000,000. At the same time, in September 1997, company also changed its name to eBay replacing AuctionWeb. This name too came to life by chance as Omidyar had established a group called Echo Bay Technology Group which held AuctionWeb and was trying to register the domain echobay.com, but the domain was not available as it was registered by a gold mining company called Echo Bay Mines, then Omidyar had to shorten the name and decide it will be "eBay.com."

Benchmark Capital, a venture capital firm, invested $6.7 million in eBay in 1997.

In March 1998, Meg Whitman was appointed as the president and CEO of eBay. There were total 30 employees who were working for the company and had already achieved a total of half a million users mark with total revenue reaching at $4.7 million in US. On September 21, 1998, eBay was opened for public investments which prompted Omidyar and Skoll to stand in a line of Billionaires. Initial share price of eBay went up to $53.50 from mere $18 on its first trading day.

Slowly and steadily, eBay expanded their range of auction, while before it was mostly collectibles, it started with other categories of products which could be sold and it proved as the right decision to increase the business of the company. Company also acquired IBazar in February 2002, a European auction website founded in 199. As they went on an acquiring spree, on October 14 2002, they also purchased PayPal.

By 2008, eBay had become a worldwide sale organization rather than just limited to US with around 15,000 employees worldwide and more than 100 million registered users. In between business also went up to new highs with total revenue touching $7.7 billion. President and CEO of eBay, Meg Whitman, resigned from eBay in 19988 to enter into politics.

In an announcement on January 23, 2008, eBay stated that Whitman would be resigning from the post of CEO and president officially on March 31, 2008. John Donahoe was appointed as the President and CEO of eBay after she left. Whitman though stayed on the Board of Directors of eBay and continuously attended meetings providing her advice to the CEO. EBay sold Skype for $2.75 billion in late 2009, but 30% equity was held back with the company.

In July 2010, XPRT ventures filed a case against eBay for a compensation of $3.8 billion accusing them to steal the information related to the patents of XPRT through their inventors. XPRT also accused eBay to use some of the important features of those in their own payment process like PayPal Buyer Credit and PayPal Pay Later.

In a process of strengthening their fashion business, Company announced to buy a German online shopping club called brand4friends for 150 $million on December 20, 2010. The deal finally processed successfully in 2011.

Website of eBay processes in sales and purchase of different categories, like appliances, décor, equipment, furnishings, collectibles, computers, vehicles, domain names, and other miscellaneous products. These items are auctioned, bought, or sold daily on eBay. Company also entered in industrial surplus business in 2006 as eBay launched a new listed category named Business & Industrial. The site also has its eBay Prohibited and Restricted Items policy which prohibits particles products or services to be listed on the site, other than that, anything can be sold and bought through the site, even intangibles and different services.

Some major international business players like IBM and Apple list their services and products on eBay for a fixed price to auction or sale. The company has also employed separate eBay sites for countries like eBay US and eBay UK. These sites allowed people to deal in their own local currencies. Software developers can join eBay Developers Program and design applications to integrate eBay through the eBay API. Over 15,000 programmers were working on eBay Developers Program in June 2005 and also there multiple companies which create their own eBay compatible applications.

Company keeps a close eye on any violated advertisement on the site. There have been many instances when there have been controversies on items put on eBay by the users. Company removes any auction or sale purchase offer which violates their terms and conditions.

Company started accepting payments only through PayPal accounts by August 2007 on its "Video Games" and "Health & Beauty" categories. Some more categories for PayPal only payments were added on January 10, 2008. These categories are "Computing > Software", "Consumer Electronics > MP3 Players", "Wholesale and Job Lots > Mobile and Home Phones", and "Business, Office and Industrial > Industrial Supply/ MRO".

Company also opened a new site called eBay express in April 2006. The site was created to like a standard shopping site to show products for US consumers with US addresses, but this site was closed 2 years later in 2008. Some selected products from eBay were shown on eBay express. This site contained a cart where buyers could purchase from several sellers. UK version of eBay express was launched in—October 2006 and was closed on January 29, 2008. It was also launched in Germany in 2006 and that too was closed in 2008.

Company held an eBay Developer's Conference in 2008 where they announced to sell Selling Manager Applications program (SM Apps). By using this program, developers could integrate their applications into the eBay.com interface directly. Members of eBay who have subscribed for Sales Manager can also subscribe for these applications made by the developers. The company has been under several controversies as well, such as cases of fraud and necessity of PayPal payments.

Site also applies some prohibitions for the users to auction and list the items because at the start it was not regulated and company had to face many problems. So, eBay made eBay Terms and Conditions which take care of regional laws and regulations for their country-specific sites. There are more than 100 categories which have been banned to b e listed on eBay.

There categories are tobacco, alcohol, drugs and drug paraphernalia, Nazi paraphernalia, bootleg recordings, firearms and ammunition, police and emergency service vehicular warning equipment, used underwear and dirty used clothing forged, illegal, stolen, or confidential documents, human parts and remains, live animals, certain copyrighted works or trademarked items, lottery tickets, sweepstakes tickets, or any other gambling items, military hardware such as working weapons or explosive, enriched uranium, plutonium, and other fissile material, sexually oriented adult material, child pornography, materials deemed obscene, including bestiality, necrophilia, rape, coprophilia, and incest, used sex toys, services including any sexual activity, links to sites that contain prohibited items, adult products that are delivered digitally, virtual items from massively multiplayer online games, restrictions that vary by country, Ivory products, knives, other than cutlery, are prohibited in the UK following media pressure about the sale of items assessed by police to be "illegal," and many other items are either wholly prohibited or restricted in some manner.

Website has three listing formats to show items for sell and purchase. First is "Auction-style listings" though which sellers can put their items for a fixed number of days which starts from a minimum reserve price. By "Fixed price format" sellers display out immediate the selling items with a "Buy It Now" tag. Any user who pays that price will be owner of the product without further bids. "Fixed price format with best offer" makes seller to choose an offer which is the best in terms of price, but if seller is not satisfied with the best offer, seller can also give a counter offer.

The success of eBay as a sale site has attracted many economist to research on user behavior towards the market. As eBay is a populated site and there are thousands of deals happening daily, it gives specialists enough data to work with and allows them to compare the results from previous similar analyzation.

JEFF BEZOS, FOUNDER OF AMAZON.COM

Jeffrey Preston Bezos who is also known as "Jeff" Bezos was born in Albuquerque, New Mexico, on January 12, 1964. Bezos is the founder, president, CEO, and chairman of the Amazon.com. Bezos is a Tau Beta Pi graduate from Princeton University and before founding Amazon, in 1994, Bezos he worked in D. E. Shaw & Co. as a financial analyst.

Bezos was born in the family of Jacklyn Gise Jorgensen and Ted Jorgensen. Bezos' maternal grandfather had a total of 25,000 areas of ranch in Cotulla and was a regional director of the US Atomic Energy Commission in Albuquerque. They were settled in Texas many years ago. Bezos' maternal grandfather was retired to work in the ranch. As a child he spent most of the time in summers working with his maternal grandfather. He had a high curiosity about mechanical settings at an early age and used to do different things with machines and instruments like screw driver and crib.

Bezos' mother was a teenager when he was born in Albuquerque. The marriage of his mother to his father only lasted for a year and then they broke up. She again married to Miguel Bezos when Jeff was 5 years old. Miguel was Cuba-born who immigrated to the United States alone at the age of 15. Miguel studied at the University of Albuquerque. Miguel after marrying Jacklyn legally adopted Jeff. They moved to Houston, Texas after the marriage where Miguel worked as an engineer for Exxon. From 4th to 6th grade, Jeff studied at River Oaks Elementary, Houston.

Bezos' scientific interests were obvious from an early age when he created an electric alarm to maintain his room's privacy from his younger brother.

He started working on science project and created a laboratory in the garage of his parents. When his family shifted to Miami, Florida, he took admission in Miami Palmetto Senior High School. While he was still studying in high school, he also started going to the University of Florida to attend the Student Science Training Program. These classes helped him in getting a Silver Knight Award in 1982. Though he completed "summa cum laude, Phi Beta Kappa" with a Bachelor of Science degree in electrical engineering and computer science, but before that he had started attending Princeton University to study physics, but his real ambition was to be a computer person, so he left physics after some time. Carnegie Mellon University awarded him with honorary doctorate in Science and Technology from in 2008.

Bezos also worked on Wall Street in the computer science after he passed from Princeton University in 1986. He also worked for a company Fitel and built a network for international trade. Then Bezos worked for Bankers Trust, becoming a vice-president. He also worked for D. E. Shaw & Co. after that.

He wrote Amazon business plan while on a cross country drive from New York to Seattle in 1994 and set up his company in his garage at the same time. He became one of the highly known dot-com business entrepreneur in US with the advent of amazon.com. He started a human spaceflight startup company in 2004 with the name "Blue Origin."

Bezos holds 20% shares of Amazon, though his salary as a CEO is not huge around $81,840 as of 2010, but he also got $1.6 million for his personal security. Bezos' estimated worth right now is $18.1 billion.

Bezos concentrates a lot on process of a business and is notoriously known for this. Conde Nast has written on his portfolio.com that "he is at once a happy-go-lucky mogul and a notorious micromanager, an executive who wants to know about everything from contract minutiae to how he is quoted in all Amazon press releases."

Time magazine names named him Person of the Year in 1999. In 2008, US News & World Report selected him as one of the Best Leaders in US.

He established Amazon.com, Inc. in 1994 which is a multinational e-commerce company based in US with head quarters in Seattle, Washington. As of January 2010, Amazon.com has become the largest online retailer in the United States.

The site Amazon.com, was put online in 1995. Amazon is not the original name for the company. The company replaced the original name Cadabra, Inc., which used to sound like "Cadaver," so they changed its name to Amazon River, one of the largest rivers in the world. Amazon.com was an online bookstore to start with, but they soon understand the potential and expanded it to different products like DVDs, CDs, MP3 downloads, computer software, video games, electronics, apparel, furniture, food, and toys. Country-specific websites have also been established by Amazon, Inc. for countries like Japan, China, Canada, United Kingdom, Italy, Franc, Germany, France, Italy, and Austria. Amazon also ships their products to some certain countries.

In 1995, when Bezos founded the site of Amazon.com, he described it as a "regret minimization framework." He himself said he had a regret of not taking benefits of Internet revolution and make money through it. According to company facts, it is reported that Bezos planned about Amazon while driving with his wife from New York to Seattle, though there not many evidence that this story is true. Another story says that Bezos took a flight from New York to Texas and from Texas he went to Seattle by driving a car which he had taken from one of his family members.

Starting as an online book store, Amazon provided large number and variety of books online. The number of books went more than 200,000. The logo of Amazon which is an arrow leading from A to Z indicates the goal for which Amazon is working that is to have products of every alphabet in the store to satisfy customers of every age. In an interview Bezos revealed that "We not only help readers find books, we also help books find readers, with personalized recommendations based on the patterns we see. I remember one of the first times this struck me. The main book on the page was on Zen. There were other suggestions for Zen books, and in the middle of those was a book on how to have a clutter-free desk. That's not something that a human editor would have ever picked. But statistically, the people who were interested in the Zen books also wanted clutter-free desks. The computer is blind to the fact that these things are dissimilar in some way that's important to humans. It looks right through that and says yes, try this. And it works." [8]

Company had come to life in 1994 while services started next year with the sale of its first book through amazon.com in July 1995. The firs sold book of Amazon was "Fluid Concepts and Creative Analogies: Computer Models of the Fundamental Mechanisms of Thought" written by Douglas Hofstadter. Office of Amazon was shifted to Delaware in 1996. On May 15 1997, Amazon started trading under NASDAQ stock exchange with its first public issue at an starting price of $18 per share and used trading symbol of AMZN, in late 90s, the value of share went down to $1.50 because of three stock splits.

On May 12, 1997, a lawsuit was filed against Amazon by Barnes and Noble. They alleged Amazon for their false claim to be "The world's largest bookstore." They said "It isn't a bookstore at all. It's a book broker." Amazon later settled the case outside the court. On October 16, 1998, Walmart also filed a suit against Amazon and alleged Amazon hired former Walmart executive to know the secrets of Walmart. This issue was also settled out of court and as a result, Walmart enforced some work restrictions on former Walmart executives.

Amazon had derived a unique and strange business plan to start with that is to survive and not hope for profits in its first 5 years. Growth was slow and that prompted stockholder to complain about the progress and lack of profitability of the company and at the same time, company faced biggest slump in the business that is when dot-com bubble was burst, but company did not go off the boil. They managed it well and persisted with it. Their perseverance resulted in the profit in 2001. They earned $5 million or 1 cent per share of profit. Though it was not a huge margin of revenue for such a large organization but it showed the potential in the business. In 1999, Bezos was named as Person of the Year by Time magazine for his big contribution in success of Amazon as an online shopping business.

---

[8]   http://www.wired.com/wired/archive/13.01/bezos.html

Amazon.com has acquired a series of ventures to expand its business and the list of acquisition is long. These acquisitions have really Amazon to make it popular in different areas of the world and helped cement its place the largest online shopping organization. They acquired a UK online book retailer named Bookpages.co.uk in 1998, which later turned into Amazon UK on October 15, 1998. In 1999, Amazon bought several different firms like Internet Movie Database (IMDb), Exchange.com, Cambridge, Massachusetts-based PlanetAll which is a reminder service, Sunnyvale-based Junglee.com which is an XML-based data mining startup Alexa Internet, and Accept.com.

They acquired CD Now, an online music retailer in 2003. A Chinese e-commerce website Joyo.com was acquired in 2004. In 2005, they bought a print on demand company, BookSurge, in 2005, an eBook software company, Mobipocket.com, and CreateSpace.com aka CustomFlix a Scotts Valley, California-based distributor of on-demand DVDs. They also acquired a Madison, Wisconsin-based retailer of designer clothing and accessories for women, called Shopbop in 2006.

In 2007, Amazon purchased dpreview.com, a digital photography review website based in London and the largest independent publisher of audio books, Brilliance Audio, in the United States. Again in 2008, they acquired quite a few firms like Audible.com, Fabric.com, Box Office Mojo, AbeBook, Shelfari, bought 40% stake in LibraryThing, owned Bookfinder.com, Gojaba.com, and FillZ, and Reflexive Entertainment.

Amazon acquired Zappos and Lexcycle, an online shoe and apparel retailer, in 2009. They acquired Touchco, Woot, Quidsi, Buyvip, and Amie Street in 2010. In 2011, Amazon took over Lovefilm in 2011.

In 2004, Amazon launched a new company to focus on researching and building innovative technology named A9.com. Other than that, an e-commerce brand endless.com was also spun off in 2007.

Amazon also hosts CDNOW.com. They also had a coalition with ToysRUs.com until June 30, 2006, when anyone who typed ToysRUs. com opened as amazon.com page of Toys & Games automatically, but this deal was canceled due to a lawsuit. A website for Borders bookstores was also hosted by Amazon but was closed in 2008.

On another note, Amazon.com also hosts and operates websites for several companies such as Target, Sears Canada, Lacoste, Benefit Cosmetics, Mothercare, bebe Stores, Marks & Spencer, and Timex. Amazon also facilitates a unified multichannel platform for its client companies like Marks & Spencer of UK merchants, UK entity Benefit Cosmetics, Mothercare, and edeals.com so that customers can contact smoothly to their retail websites, phone-based customer service agents, or standalone in-store terminals. Shop@AOL of AOL is also hosted by Amazon Web Services.

In 2003, the net income of Amazon was $35 million which went up to $588 million in 2004, $359 million in 2005, and $190 million in 2006 where they also spent $662 million charge for R&D. Amazon also had $1.8 billion in 2006, negative $1.4 billion in 2007, negative $730 million in 2008, and $172 million in 2009, in retained earnings. Annual profits through revenues expansion of the product categories and services also increased from $3.9 billion in 2002 to $10.7 billion by 2006.

Amazon made its entry S&P 500 index on November 21, 2005. Three years later, on March 26, 2010, it entered in S&P 100 index as well. By March 26, 2010, Amazon had left Target Corporation, Barnes and Noble, Home Depot, Best Buy, and Costco in higher market cap, and only Walmart was ahead among brick and mortar retailer business organizations.

Amazon.com has also established several software development centers, customer service centers offices, and fulfillment centers all over the world like North America, Latin America, Europe, and Asia.

Old head quarter of the Amazon.com was in the former Veterans Hospital building in Beacon Hill, Seattle. While the global head quarter of the company is established in South Lake Union neighborhood, Seattle.

By 2008, company website domain amazon.com had achieved a mark of 615 million visitors annually which is double to what walmart.com had. There are around 65 million users visiting the US website of Amazon per month. They have also increased their server capacity to a huge amount to counter excessive traffic on the site and keep it fast and up to date with advanced hardware and software updates. They update the servers during December Christmas holiday season every year.

Users can write reviews on the products which reviewers can rate and give rating from one to five on a rating scale. These rating stars tell you the state and quality of the product as one star means a poor product and five stars means a fantastic product. There is also a badging option which shows the real name of the reviewer. This also indicates how the reviewer has performed and how popular the review is. Giving ratings to the review is also possible, which indicates if the review has been helpful for the users or not.

Amazon also manages the submission of review and monitors them for any abuses. Negative reviews and comments are allowed. An author Robert Spector, who wrote the book Amazon.com, says in that book, "When publishers and authors asked Bezos why amazon.com would publish negative reviews, he defended the practice by claiming that amazon.com was taking a different approach. We want to make every book available, the good, the bad, and the ugly, to let truth loose'." Though there have been accusations that negative reviews and comments related to Scientology have been deleted even if they comply with the Amazon comments guidelines.

Amazon.com was also selling print on demand books most of which were reproduction of Wikipedia articles and was criticized by blogosphere and German-speaking press for this. An American company, Books LLC along with German publisher VDM, which has three Mauritian subsidiaries named Alphascript Publishing, Betascript Publishing, and Fastbook Publishing produced these books. However, Amazon did not accept the claims which were raised by blog writers as well as the customers, to take all these out from their shelves. Amazon.com had started listing these books in the site catalog since 2007 when they had collaborated with VDM Publishing.

Amazon was also hosting websites related to WikiLeaks, a website which created storm in politics and diplomacy between the countries. Though it was not clear whether they asked website to quit Amazon or it left the space itself. As on December 1, 2010, Amazon stopped hosting the website. According to New York Times, "Senator Joseph I. Lieberman, independent of Connecticut, said Amazon had stopped hosting the WikiLeaks site on Wednesday after being contacted by the staff of the Homeland Security and Governmental Affairs Committee."

Amazon later held a press release according to which they did not stopped wikileaks.org because of political pressures or government inquiries, rather the step was taken due to violation of the rules and regulations of Amazon as wikileaks.org was displaying and storing material which could affect privacy of government, politicians, and other people and they were not authorized to do that.

WikiLeaks founder, Julian Assange, said this step was not in the best interest of public and journalism and violated the human rights of freedom of speech.

Then Daniel Ellsberg who is famous for several of his acts like leaking the Pentagon Papers during the Vietnam War wrote a public letter regarding this incident saying that, "he was disgusted by Amazon's cowardice and servility which is similar to China's control of information and deterrence of whistle-blowing." He urged public to boycott Amazon immediately.

REID G. HOFFMAN,
FOUNDER OF LINKEDIN

Reid G. Hoffman, the co-founder of LinkedIn, is an American entrepreneur and angel investor who was born on August 5, 1967. Hoffman co-founded LinkedIn which is a social network that is used extensively for business connections and job search.

Born in Stanford, California, Reid Hoffman then grew up in Berkeley, California. He went to The Putney School to attend high school. He completed his graduation from Stanford University in 1990. At Stanford University, he won Marshall Scholarship as well as Dinkelspiel Award. He completed his degree of B.S. in Symbolic Systems. He then went to Oxford University in 1993 and earned an M.A. in philosophy.

According to Hoffman, he was eyeing great opportunities and impressive career in academics where he can leave an impact through his knowledge and skills, but it was not to be his destiny and then he turned to entrepreneurship which provided him a better and bigger platform to express himself. He, himself, said it once that after the completion of graduation from Stanford, he wanted to be a professor, but he realized that this is not going to be his destination. He thought as an academic person, his reach can be very limited. He wanted to do something big where many a people will know him through his ventures and thoughts.

Hoffman then started his journey towards his ambition of a career in business and entrepreneurship to leave a bigger impact on world stage. He first worked at Apple Computer and then Fujitsu where he was in product management department. After than he co-founded SocialNet.com which was the first company he launched and was an online dating portal.

While Hoffman was running SocialNet, he also became a member of the board of directors at PayPal when it was founded. Paypal is an electronic money transmission service, but after some time, he started working as a full-time employee at PayPal. PayPal was then acquired by eBay in 2002, at that time he was the Executive Vice President of the company. At PayPal, he used to manage the external relationships as well as payments infrastructure such as with VISA, MasterCard, ACH, and WellsFargo. He also took the responsibility of Business Development such as with eBay and Intuit, Government stuffs like Regulatory and Judicial, and used to look after the legal issues as well.

LinkedIn was co-founded by Hoffman in December 2002. The founding team members of LinkedIn are from Paypal and Socialnet.com. Their names are as follows; Allen Blue, Chris Saccherilt, Eric Ly, Yan Pujante, Jean-Luc Vaillant, Ian McNish, Lee Hower, David Eves, Stephen Beitzel, and Konstantin Guericke. LinkedIn was the first of its kind of a social service which was business-oriented and was giving the opportunities to professional to connect to each other and was also helping job search.

He remained CEO of LinkedIn for first 4 years since its inception. Then he became Chairman and President of Products in February 2007. Right now, he serves as an Executive chairman at LinkedIn. LinkedIn currently has a huge membership number that are around 100 million and is spread in more than 200 countries. Tiger Global Management purchased 1% shares of LinkedIn in July 2010 and the value of the company was estimated at $2 billion.

IPO of LinkedIn came out on May 19, 2011, in which Hoffman holds a total worth of 2.34 billion dollars estimated, and other than these numbers, he is also a partner in Greylock Partners.

Jeff Weiner is the CEO of LinkedIn right now. He was with Yahoo! Inc. before and worked as an executive. LinkedIn gets funding support from various support partners such as Sequoia Capital, Bessemer Venture Partners, Bain Capital Ventures, Greylock, and European Founders Fund. The company had reached to a total of $103 million of investment till January 2011. Sequoia Capital started the series of investment in the company in 2003. Sequoia Capital, Greylock Partners, and other venture capital firms bought a 5% stake in LinkedIn in 2008 for $53 million with total value of the company which was estimated at approximately $1 billion at that time.

LinkedIn opened a head quarter in Europe in June 2010 that was established in Dublin, Ireland. Tiger Global Management LLC also acquired 1% shares of the company for $20 million in July 2010. They had estimated overall value of the company at approximately $2 billion. LinkedIn acquired Mspoke in August 2010. This acquisition was done for an undisclosed amount and this was the first time they made a deal where they acquired a whole company.

The motive behind this step was to make LinkedIn more interesting and interactive for users. They were trying to increase the activities of the users not only for finding jobs but also to increase premium subscription ratio which was hanging at 1%. Silicon Valley Insider gave the company a #10 position in a total of 100 companies in October 2010 for most valuable startups. Total worth of LinkedIn was calculated around $1.575 billion in private markets in December 2010.

LinkedIn IPO that was filed on January 27, 2011, came out to public on May 19, 2011. Shares of the company were priced at $45 to start with, but the price was increased up to $122 on its first trading day. When first day trading was ended, it had gained around 109%. In the post bubble era, LinkedIn IPO proved to be the fifth largest first day gainer.

Hoffman has also been involved in angel investing and after the PayPal was acquired by eBay, He became one of the most successful angel investor in Silicon Valley. Venture capitalist David Sze regarded him as arguably the most successful angel investor of the decade then. He had invested around 80 angel investments in that time period, all in technology companies of the Valley. Hoffman also joined Greylock Partners in 2010.

David Kirkpatrick wrote a book "The Facebook Effect" in which he mentioned that Hoffman helped introducing Mark Zuckerberg to Peter Thiel, which prompted Thiel to shell out $500,000 as an angel investment in the company. Hoffman along with Thiel helped in development of the Facebook through their investments.

Hoffman also joined the board of directors in Zynga where he personally invested in first round of funding of the company. The Six Degrees Patent is also co-owned by Hoffman and Zynga's CEO Mark Pincus. If we believe SecondShares.com, Zynga's value is estimated at about $5 billion.

Hoffman's has also invested in several other companies such as shopkick, Wikia, OneKingsLane, Permuto, Technetto, SixApart, Last.fm, thesixtyone, Kongregate, Tagged, Knewton, IronPort, Care.com, Flickr, Digg, Nanosolar, and Ping.fm, etc.

Hoffman has also been a big supporter of philosophy of Philanthropy and works on the boards of Do Something, an organization which works for young people. Other than that, He also serves Kiva.org which is a micro-finance organization. He supports Mozilla for his development works, they developed Firefox. Hoffman is also associated with Endeavor Global. This international non-profit organization works in helping and supporting new potential entrepreneurs in the market.

The rivals of LinkedIn are Viadeo and Xing and they have 30 million and 10 million users, respectively, but they are still far behind LinkedIn in terms of user numbers and with 100 million users, LinkedIn has made its own niche among professional users. With one user joining every second, LinkedIn is now growing faster than ever. Popularity of LinkedIn can be seen by the number of users it has from US and Europe.

Around 50 million users are from US alone, while Europe contributes about 11 million users, but still compared to these two, LinkedIn markets are left behind by Indian users in terms of growth of the network. As of 2009, LinkedIn had the fastest growth in India with 3 million users. LinkedIn has scored 30% adoption rate per capita in Netherlands, which is just behind USA. LinkedIn also achieved a target of 4 million users in UK recently and it also has reached to 1 million users in Spain

The site has an option named "Connections" through which a user can maintain a list of contacts with whom user interacts more often regarding their professional or personal issues. The site is made purposefully to help registered users systematically. A user can send invitation to the people user knows through e-mail to join the site and become a part of the connection.

The site also applies some restrictions to the user for fail invites, when recipients select "I don't know." This can have negative consequences on user's account which can be prohibited to send more invitations after five such "IDK" events. After that, a member can only send invites by providing recipient's e-mail address.

LinkedIn can be used for job search and to create business opportunities by using your own contacts or by using other users' contact who is in contact with you on the network. Employers use LinkedIn to use job candidates for their organizations on the network and give the opportunities to able people to contact them. Users can also upload their photos for identification. Users find several companies listed on the site which he can follow and get to know about any job opportunities via notifications. Bookmark options are also available for users to save the jobs for which they want to apply.

Users can also search for the companies they want to work with and know who can provide them the best platform to show their skills and help them grow. As the user types the company's name in the search option, LinkedIn shows the company statistics. It includes the number of employees categorized by male and female employees, jobs available in the company, and the most number of common designations in the company. The search will also show company's location along with headquarters, other important offices, and branches. User will also get to know about the present and former employees of the company.

Another feature which is pretty similar to Yahoo Answers is LinkedIn Answers in which users can ask questions from the LinkedIn community. This feature is different than Yahoo Answers in terms of questions asked here, which are mostly business-related questions, and this facility is available for free. LinkedIn Answers also show the identity of the people who are asking and answering the questions.

LinkedIn Polls is also an additional feature associated with the site, which gives users a chance to give their verdict on a certain topic through voting. LinkedIn can also be accessed via mobile. The mobile site though provides less number of features than the original site and it was launched n February

2008. The mobile site can be accessed in six different languages such as English, German, Japanese, Chinese, French, and Spanish.

LinkedIn DirectAds were launched in 2008 for sponsored advertising. In October 2008, LinkedIn announced business-to-business research plans through its social network of 30 million professional users and is eyeing for a revenue model through social Network research. One more feature was added in LinkedIn in October 2008 and that was called "applications platform" to allow users to add other online services to their profile. Some of those online services were Amazon Reading List, Tripit, WordPress, Six Apart, and Type Pad.

In November 2010, LinkedIn started showing products and services on respective company profile pages. This allowed LinkedIn users to write reviews about the products and services. LinkedIn also bought a mobile app maker, CardMunch in January 2011. CardMunch provides scanning facility of business cards and converts them into contacts and LinkedIn is planning to include this function in their services. Interest groups are another integral part of LinkedIn, and till Match 24, 2011, there were 870,612 existing groups. Most of these groups are related to employment which covered professional and career issues.

These groups are moderated and edited by group owners and a limited discussion can be done with other users. This works pretty much like a sensor board. Because a wide range of user can access this service, this in turn attracts spamming as well and these groups come across a huge number of spammers and there are also some firms who especially provide these kinds of spamming services. Though LinkedIn has developed a few techniques to deal with the spamming issues, it is still a big concern for them. Different groups are categorized as private, open only for members, or open for all to read but positing is allowed for members only.

LinkedIn has restrictions in some countries according to US export and re-export control Laws, and for this reason, in 2009, LinkedIn services in Syria were abandoned by the company, as company's servers stopped responding to the IP addresses originating from Syria. Other than that, Iran, Sudan, and Cuba are the countries which are not available in LinkedIn's list of countries for selection by the users. The name of North

Korea was also supposed to be removed from the list but till April 2010, it was still there.

According to some news in the media, LinkedIn was blocked in China in February 2011 because of possibilities of "Jasmine Revolution" spreading through LinkedIn as it was easy to access Twitter by dissidents through LinkedIn and Twitter had already suffered a block before in China, though this block of LinkedIn remained for only a day.

ELON MUSK & PETER THIEL, FOUNDER OF PAYPAL

PETER THIEL

Peter Thiel is an American entrepreneur and a hedge fund manager. He is a libertarian and venture capitalist of German descent. He co-founded PayPal with Elon Musk and Max Levchin and was the CEO of PayPal. He currently is a president of Clarium Capital which is a global macro hedge fund. He has $700 million worth of assets under management. He is also a managing partner in The Founders Fund which has $275 million venture capital fund.

He launched The Founders Fund with Ken Howery and Luke Nosek in 2005. Thiel also invested in Facebook at initial stages and is now a member of board of directors at Facebook which is one of the most popular social networking sites now. In 2010, Thiel was ranked at #365 on the Forbes 400 list. He was supposed to have a net worth of US$1.5 billion. Now his Facebook shares alone are of worth US$1.7 billion

Peter Andreas Thiel was born in Frankfurt am Main, West Germany, in 1967. He was brought up in Foster City, California. Peter Thiel now lives in San Francisco, California. Peter Thiel was a US-rated Chess Master. At one time, he was one of the highest ranked under-21 players in the country. As an undergraduate, he studied 20th century philosophy at Stanford University. He is a libertarian and he initiated The Stanford Review which is now a main conservative/libertarian newspaper of the university. He completed his B.A. in Philosophy in 1989 from Stanford University. He then pursued J.D. from Stanford Law School in 1992.

Thiel also worked as a clerk at 11ᵗʰ Circuit Court of Appeals under Judge J.L. Edmondson. He also worked in trading of derivatives for Credit Suisse Group from 1993 to 1996. In 1996, he founded a multi-strategy fund called Thiel Capital Management.

Thiel co-founded the PayPal and launched its IPO on February 15, 2002, which was then bought by eBay for $1.5 billion later in the same year. He had 3.7% shares in PayPal which was worth about $55 million at that time. After the deal of PayPal, a global macro hedge fund, Clarium, was launched by Thiel with a purpose of pursuing a global macro strategy.

Two trade magazines MarHedge and Absolute Return awarded Clarium as a global macro fund of the year in 2005. A famous writer Steve Drobny wrote a full chapter in his book "Inside the House of Money" about Thiel's approach to investing. He predicted that US dollar will be weakened in 2003 which was proved to be right. He also gained high returns on increasing values of US dollar and energy in 2005.

In 2004, Thiel spoke about migration of dot-com bubble to financial sector and he proved right when financial crisis happened from 2007 to 2010 across the world which started originally from USA. He also talked about vulnerable financial health of General Electric and WalMart.

Along with that, he observed about a real estate bubble at the same time and he proved it when he backed away from a deal of buying Martha Stewart's Manhattan duplex for $ 7 million in 2003-2004. In the same year later in 2004 the property sold for $ 6.65 million, and was then kept in the market by the owner in early 2010 at $15 million but was not purchased by anyone, it was not even sold when the price was reduced to $13.9 million.

One of the main features of Thiel's investment is that, he always invests in such companies that give him better returns. For example, his early investment in Facebook in late 2004, helped Facebook to come up as an individual concern and develop as a major social networking site. He invested $500,000 as an angel investor in Facebook for 10.2% shares. Other than that, Thiel also made several other early stage investments to help the startups to grow as an individual business. Most of these investments were done through his venture capital fund. Some of these companies are Slide, CapLinked, LinkedIn, IronPort, Rypple, Friendster, Rapleaf, Joyent, Geni.com, Palantir Technologies, Clickable Inc, Vator, Yammer, Powerset, Yelp, and Inc.

Some of these above mentioned companies are founded by Thiel's former PayPal partners. Slide was founded by Max Levchin. Reid Hoffman founded LinkedIn. Jeremy Stoppelman founded Yelp. Founder of Geni. com and Yammer is David Sacks while Xero was started by Rod Drury. An amazing fact was reported in Fortune magazine about the PayPal alumni that they invested approximately $30 billion of total sum in dozens of startups.

Peter Thiel is also called as the "Don of the PayPal Mafia." This name of his was mentioned in the same Fortune magazine article. Thiel also believes that success of the start-ups plays a huge role in low CEO salaries. His management philosophies are very highly rated by several organizations.

Thiel has also done a few shows as a commentator for CNBC with Maria Bartiromo on Closing Bell and with Becky Quick on Squawk Box. One of his interviews with Charlie Rose was shown on PBS. He got Herman Lay Award for Entrepreneurship in 2006 and honored as a Young Global leader by the World Economic Forum on a list of 250 achievers age 40 in 2007. Universidad Francisco Marroquin gave an honorary degree to Thiel on November 7, 2009.

Thiel also worked on a feature film named "Thank You for Smoking" as an executive producer in 2005. The film was based on a novel written by Christopher Buckley in 1994. Thiel has co-authored a book named "The Diversity Myth: 'Multiculturalism' and the Politics of Intolerance at Stanford" in combination with David O. Sacks in 1995. This got serious criticisms from then Stanford Provost Condoleezza Rice who later became National Security Advisor of President George W. Bush. Thiel has also written articles for First Thing, The Wall Street Journal, Forbes, and Policy Review.

Thiel anchored a meeting related to the future of science and technology in December 2010. Many successful Silicon Valley entrepreneurs attended that meeting where Thiel gave an idea of investing in futuristic projects to elevate the living condition of the people in society. Right now, Thiel is writing a book in company of Max Levchin and Garry Kasparov named "The Blueprint" on concept of revival of world innovation. The book will come out in February 2012 and will be published by W. W. Norton & Company.

Thiel backed the Singularity Challenge donation drive of the Singularity Institute for Artificial Intelligence and gave $100,000 of matching funds. In addition, he served the advisory board of Institute. Thiel participated in Singularity Summit at Stanford in May 2006 on behalf of the institute.

Thiel also promoted an anti-aging research done by Methuselah Mouse Prize foundation and donated $3.5 millions in September 2006. He is a great supporter of biological science advancement through new researches to increase the longevity of life and good health. He supported Dr. De Grey, a biologist, who was running a research on aging process. He provided $200,000 of match funds for the annual Singularity Challenge donation drive in May 2007.

Thiel is heavy donator which he proved again when he pledged $500,000 to the new Seasteading Institute on April 15, 2008. The director of the institute was Patri Friedman who had a mission to establish permanent, autonomous ocean communities for experimentation and innovation on diverse social, political, and legal systems. After this, subsequent grant of $250,000 and an additional $100,000 of funds were also donated to the institute in February 2010.

Thiel then announced a Thiel Fellowship on September 29, 2010. Through this fellowship, $100,000 each were given to minimum 20 people of age not more than 20, to encourage them to quit college and start their own ventures. Thiel also supports a committee called Committee to Protect Journalists so that reporters and journalists can work freely without any fear. This community works for protecting the rights and lives of the journalists.

The Bilderberg Group, which he is a member of, is a group of government leaders and high profile businessman who organize meeting every year to talk about world issues behind closed doors. This meeting has been so secret that even media do not get to know anything out of it. Thiel is a libertarian and in 2004, he advised many free-market think tanks, including the Pacific Research Institute in San Francisco. He is a believer of liberal policy regarding markets and thinks that open markets can be more beneficial for people.

According to Thiel, as his political beliefs are libertarian, he supported and promoted Ron Paul for Presidential elections in December 2007. In an article, he wrote for the Cato Institute, he said "I no longer believe that freedom and democracy are compatible." Later, he explained his beliefs and concepts of politics in the next article where he wrote, "While I do not think any class of people should be disenfranchised, I have little hope that voting will make things better."

Peter Thiel claims that he does not believe in "unacceptable compromise politics." He then wrote another piece of article for Oslo Freedom Forum in which he wrote "We tend to like a government very much when we believe we are among its net winners. That makes it very hard to think clearly about whether any of its laws are just or unjust. And because power corrupts, any state unchecked by vigorous public scrutiny and a free press will attempt to become the judge in its own cause and the intermediary of all human interaction."

In 2009, it was reported that Thiel helped a college student James O'Keefe who made a satirical video named "Taxpayers Clearing House." This video exposed the politics behind the Wall Street bailout. Allegedly, Peter Thiel supported the student financially in making that video. James O'Keefe later produced another video named "ACORN undercover sting videos."

Thiel also worked for gay-rights and helped foundations such as the American Foundation for Equal Rights and GOProud. For the governorship of California, Thiel supported former eBay CEO, Meg Whitman, in 2010, though Meg Whitman could not succeed in his ambitions. Meg Whitman was the CEO of eBay when Thiel sold PayPal to eBay. In that campaign, he spent $25,900 net.

A film named "The Social Network" was made on a subject related to web and online revolution which also had a character similar to Peter Thiel that was depicted by Wallace Langham.

ELON MUSK

Elon Musk was born in South Africa on June 28, 1971. He is an American engineer and entrepreneur. Elon was brought up in South Africa. He is also known as a philanthropist of South African-Canadian heritage. He co-founded PayPal, Tesla Motors, and SpaceX. Right now, he serves SpaceX as a CEO and CTO. In addition, he is a CEO and Product Architect at Tesla Motors. He also serves as the Chair person of SolarCity. Musk got real popularity for inventing first electric sports car named Tesla Roadster. This car was considered as first real production electric sports car. He also invented a private successor to the Space Shuttle, called Dragon. Along with that, he co-founded PayPal, world's largest online payment system.

Elon Musk's father was an engineer in South Africa and his mother was of Canadian origin who worked as a Nutritionist and model. He learnt programming by himself when he bought his first computer at the age of 10. He completed his first commercial software by the age of 12 which he sold for $500. The software's name was Blaster which was a space game.

He passed high school from Pretoria Boys High School and then, he left his home at the age of 17, in the year 1988 to spend his life in better way rather than doing a compulsory service in the military in South Africa. Musk quoted "I do not have an issue with serving in the military per se, but serving in the South African army suppressing black people just did not seem like a really good way to spend time." He then moved to USA and said that "It is where great things are possible."[9]

Musk went to western Canada as his mother was born in Regina, Saskatchewan, Canada, and he had many of his relatives living there, so it was a viable option for him to shift there. In June 1989, he immigrated to western Canada. He first started working in his cousin's wheat farm in

---

[9] Belfiore, Michael (2007). "Chapter 7: "Orbit on a Shoestring"". *Rocketeers*. HarperCollins. pp. 166-195

Swift Current, Saskatchewan, and he had to work in vegetable patches and cleaned out grain bins.

He also worked in British Columbia in a lumber mill where he cleaned out boilers and also cut the logs by chainsaw. After that, he worked in computer department of bank situated in Toronto. While working in the bank, he also aspired for the higher studies and applied to Queen's University.

Later, in 1992, he got a scholarship to study business and physics at the University of Pennsylvania. He then moved from Canada to Pennsylvania. He completed his undergraduate as well as second bachelor degree from Wharton School affiliated by University of Pennsylvania. He always took inspirations from science innovators like Thomas Edison and Nikola Tesla and always wanted to achieve something significant in his life, but he only had undergraduate degrees to his name which were never a great achievement for any one, so then he chose three areas to work on Internet, clean energy, and space.

To achieve his goals, he decided to go for a graduate program in 1995 at Stanford University here his subjects were applied physics and materials science, but it was not he actually wanted to do and therefore, he dropped the university in 2 days and started Zip2 in which his brother Kimbal Musk helped him. Through this service, they developed online content publishing software. This software helped news agencies a lot. Zip2 was then acquired by Compaq AltaVista in 1999 for US$307 million in cash. Musk then co-founded an online financial and e-mail payment service named X.com in March 1999. X.com was then merged with another company Confinity which also had PayPal in its community, a year later. X.Com's legal name was changed to PayPal in February 2001.

PayPal was bought by eBay in October 2002 for US$1.5 billion. At the time of acquisition, Musk held 11.7% shares of PayPal.

Space Exploration technologies aka SpaceX was founded by Musk in June 2002. This was his third company after Zip2 and PayPal. This company is still running under the watchful of eyes of Elon Musk who is the CEO and CTO of the company. SpaceX develops and manufactures low cost and high reliability space vehicles. Company has already launched space crafts and Dragon is first one of them. Other than that, they have developed Falcon 1 and Falcon 9 space launch rockets. On December 23, 2008, NASA gave a $1.6 billion contract to SpaceX for their Falcon 9 rocket flights. They also have a plan to send Dragon spacecraft to the International Space Station as a substitute to Space Shuttle which will stop working by 2011.

Though SpaceX has developed Falcon 9/Dragon in considering astronaut transports, but to begin with Falcon 9/Dragon will only be used for cargo transport and Soyuz will be used for astronaut transport. However, a report came out that Augustine Commission had recommended to NASA that astronaut transports should be managed by commercial companies like SpaceX. Space exploration is an ambitious plan in Musk's book for expanding the canvas for living of human being.

According to Musk, multi-planetary life is a solution for problems which we will face in the future, so the urgency is to work on these solutions and make them possible to save human species. Musk further says that "An asteroid or a super volcano could destroy us, and we face risks the dinosaurs never saw: An engineered virus, inadvertent creation of a micro black hole, catastrophic global warming or some as-yet-unknown technology could spell the end of us. Humankind evolved over millions of years, but in the last sixty years atomic weaponry created the potential to extinguish ourselves. Sooner or later, we must expand life beyond this green and blue ball—or go extinct." [10]

According to Musk, his biggest goal now is to reduce the cost of space traveling. SpaceX was founded by him and to achieve these goals he had to invest $100 million. The company is based in Hawthorne, California, and he is also a CEO of SpaceX. It has been seven years since Musk launched SpaceX and in these years, they have developed Falcon space launch vehicles and the Dragon multi-purpose spacecraft. Falcon 1 is the first liquid-fueled vehicle which launched a satellite into orbit and is developed and funded by a private organization.

---

[10]   http://www.mindovermachines.com/insight/genius-madness

The biggest achievement that SpaceX has to show is that they are the first commercial company to be chosen by NASA for their International Space Station cargo transport program. The contract value ranges from $1.6 billion to $3.1 billion, minimum to maximum respectively.

Another of Elon Musk's innovation is Tesla Motors. He is co-founder and chairman of the board and serves as head of the product design. He along with his engineers developed the design of Tesla Roadster. Tesla Roadster is considered the first viable production electric car. Saving energy and making clean energy options was one of the three goals for Musk, and with those three goals in mind, he took admission in Stanford University to do PhD in Applied Physics and Material Science. He wanted to develop ultracapacitors for the electric cars, though he could not complete his PhD, but he was continuously working to achieve from his goals that he had set for him.

He founded Tesla and managed all of the funds for its starting two funding rounds from his pocket and he still looks after the financial matters of the company. Even when financial crisis took over the market in 2008, Musk bore the responsibility of a CEO for the company. Tesla Roadster, developed by Tesla Motors is an electric sports car and exported to 31 countries. They have sold over 1800 units of the car by now. Next year, in 2012, Tesla will be coming with a new model of its electric car innovation which will be a four door S sedan. Their SUV/mini-van category vehicle Model X will also be launched in late 2011.

Toyota and Daimler are the long-term investors in Tesla, and Tesla manufactures electric powertrain systems for Daimler and Toyota for their luxurious car brands like, Smart EV and Mercedes A Class, and upcoming electric RAV4, respectively. Musk is an ambitious businessman who derived an overarching business strategy and aimed to provide electrical vehicles at low prices. His unique strategy of making Tesla Roadster worked amazingly well as he always wanted to make a sports car which can be bought by high profile people and then he could invest and earn profit in the development of other low cost electric cars for common human being.

The example for this strategy is the Model S family sedan car which has been priced half of the Tesla Roadster which is a luxurious electric sports car. For his vision and revolutionary contribution towards advanced vehicle powertrain, Musk has been compared to Henry Ford by journalists. SolarCity was started in 2006, which provides photovoltaics products and services, and was co-founded by his cousin Lyndon Rive. Elon Musk is a primary investor and a board member in the company. SolarCity is another attempt by Musk to fight against the global warming along with Tesla.

Musk Foundation was established by Elon Musk to work for the betterment of people who works on science education, pediatric health, and clean energy. Musk is a great philanthropist and is a trustee of the X Prize Foundation.

X Prize Foundation promotes renewable energy technologies. He is also the board member of several other foundations such as Stanford Engineering Advisory Board, The Planetary Society, The Space Foundation, and The National Academies Aeronautics and Space Engineering Board. Musk is also a trustee of the California Institute of Technology. In 2010, a program to donate solar power systems in disaster areas proved Musk's belief in philanthropy. Millions of dollars were spent to execute this program successfully and without the expectations of any return. There operations were done in those lone areas where SolarCity had not reached till then which showed that the program was not started for any commercial purposes. During this program, first solar power installation was done in Alabama which was hugely affected by hurricane.

Mars Oasis program was started in 2001 by Musk. This program was an experimentation of growing food crops using Martian regolith of Mars and making a greenhouse on Mars. However, that plan could not go ahead at that time because of lack of advanced space aviation technologies. For that, he then founded SpaceX to develop and invent new space travel technologies. Musk was included in a list of 20 most powerful CEO's in America in 2011 by Forbes. He was presented with a highest award for air and space technology by Federation Aeronautique Internationale in 2010. He was also given an FAI Gold Space Medal for his Falcon rocket. In 2010, he was named in top 100 most influential people in the world by Time Magazine. Esquire magazine named him one of the 75 most influential people of the 21st century.

In an interview Elon stated about the three inventions that will change the world. According to him, "One of the most important things that I think that will be invented this century, hopefully by SpaceX, is the first **fully reusable orbital rocket**. It's the fundamental invention necessary for humanity to expand to the stars and to become multiplanetary." His second invention would be, "**Rapid, low-cost, perfect DNA sequencing** will have a huge effect on humanity. Human DNA has not yet been completely decoded. The most that anyone has gotten is about 91% or 92%, and that has been with a huge numbers of errors. Trying to read our DNA is like trying to understand software code—with only 90% of the code riddled with errors. It's very difficult in that case to understand and predict what that software code is going to do." And the third invention to change the world would be, "There are a lot of people that think **viable fusion** is not possible. But fusion is the "energy forever" solution. You know all energy in the universe originates with fusion. We get our energy from the sun, so that's indirect reliance on fusion." [11]

Elon Musk got bucketful of awards and recognition for his contribution and innovations in different fields. For creating a successor to Space Shuttle, he was recognized as a "Living Legend in Aviation" by the Kitty Hawk Foundation in 2010. In 2007-2008, he was awarded with American Institute of Aeronautics and Astronautics George Low award for his contribution in space transportation. Another award he got was in 2008-2009 by National Space Society's Von Braun Trophy which he was given for the biggest achievement in space.

He was also given National Conservation Achievement award for Tesla Motors and SolarCity by the National Wildlife Federation in 2008. He was announced as the automotive executive of the year in 2010 for his contributions in Tesla motors. Entrepreneur of the year award was given by Inc Magazine in 2007. He was also awarded Honorary Doctorate by Amherst College, Massachusetts, Honorary doctorate in aerospace

---

[11]   http://globalpublicsquare.blogs.cnn.com/2011/03/17/elon-musk-on-the-3-inventions-that-will-change-the-world/

engineering from the University of Surrey, UK, and another Honorary doctorate in design from the Art Center College of Design. In a Space Foundation survey in 2010, Musk was ranked at #10 in most popular space hero.

Musk lives with his wife Talulah Riley, who is a British Actor, in Bel-Air, California. This is his second marriage and he also has five children from his ex-wife who is a Canadian-born author named Justine Musk. The Hollywood film Iron Man II was shot at Musk's SpaceX factory. Musk also had a little cameo role in that movie.

Drew Curtis
Founder of FARK.com

There are millions of websites out there in the world of internet, but out of them there are very few who make their own mark in the business and earn money out of it. Fark.com is one such name. Fark was created by Drew Curtis, and it features all the weird and funny news from all over the world. Through the years Fark has made its own mark, and the one person solely responsible for the success of the site is Drew Curtis. Since the time Curtis has founded Fark.com, it is his full time job. He has managed to make huge money out of the enterprise.

Drew Curtis was born on February 7, 1973, at Lexington, Kentucky, United States. He is the founder and administrator of Fark.com. It is a site where links of funny news can be dumped from all the websites. Along with creating the website, he is also the author of a book named *It's Not News, It's FARK: How Mass Media Tries to Pass off Crap as News* which he published in May, 2007.

In 1995, Drew Curtis did his graduation from the Luther College in Decorah, Iowa. He owned and operated an ISP based in Frankfort, Kentucky.

The history of the website Fark.com began when Curtis was studying in England in the year 1993. He used to send links back to his friends in college through mail. But he got afraid as it might annoy his friends, therefore he thought of creating a website where he can pour in the entire link. In 1997, Curtis registered his website, but started posting links on the site in 1999. The first story put up on the site was regarding a fighter pilot. Since, that time the website became very popular and is now, one of the most popular sites on the internet.

In a month, it nearly has 50 million page views. Until, 2006 Fark was receiving more than 2,000 link submissions on a daily basis. Curtis is the one who acts as a filter and selects the stories which will go on board. Although he has employed two other people for the job, but they do the link selection only when Drew is busy or he is on a run. But whenever he is at home, he is the one who is responsible for selecting all the links which would be submitted on the site.

The classified section of the blog generates to the maximum of $40,000 per annum, and it is the first indie blog to generate $ 1 million profit in a year.

Amongst many advertisers who publish their classified advertisements regularly in the website, the majority of the revenue generated comes through few major companies like Old Spice and Kawasaki. Fark.com is one amongst the 100 largest English language sites which received 4 million unique visitors in a month and 2,000 link submissions per day. Although Curtis is the creator of the website, and Fark being a million dollar enterprise, he takes home an annual salary of $60,000, and the remaining money goes to the website's legal 'war chest' and for the payment of other expenses.

While speaking to the media at a conference held in Washington, DC, which was hosted by the Poynter Institute, he stated, "The 'wisdom of the crowds' is the most ridiculous statement I've heard in my life. Crowds are dumb. It takes people to move crowds in the right direction, crowds by themselves just stand around and mutter".[12]

The business 2.0 magazine featured Curtis on its cover page in a story about successful websites, in the year 2006. He was named one of the businessmen under 40 to watch by Lexington Weekly. Curtis filed an application on November 28, 2007, to trademark the phrase "not safe for work" on Fark.com, but his application was denied.

---

[12] http://thehill.com/blogs/hillicon-valley/technology/106231-fark-creator-says-wisdom-of-crowds-is-overrated

It's Not News, It's FARK: How Mass Media Tries to Pass off Crap as News the first book published by Curtis was a bestseller. In this book he has mainly targeted the news media and how they try to manipulate stories and give it the angle of news. The book has a critical look at the news and Mass Media industry and how they use simple stories and make them news when they lack actual hard core news to publish. While running Fark. com, which basically deals with strange news stories, Drew noticed some of the specific patterns within the mass media, and how they sensationalize a simple story and give it the angle of news. This actually inspired him to write this book.

It's Not News, It's FARK is divided into eight sections. Each section deals with specific patterns which are exhibited by the mass media industry. There are specific stories or news items within each pattern, which exemplifies that specific pattern. Curtis has also listed humorous comments at the end of each example from his original website Fark.com and presented the discussion thread which covered the specific stories which the mass media considered news and published it on the websites, news papers, broadcasted or used any other means of communication for it.

The eight sections in which the book was divided were: Media Fearmongering, Unpaid Placement Masquerading as Actual Article, Headline Contradicted by Actual Article, Equal Time for Nutjobs, The Out-of-Context Celebrity Comment, Seasonal Articles, Media Fatigue and Lesser Media Space Fillers. All these sections had great humor associated with it and mocked the mass media for spreading needless information as news articles.

Curtis' book ranked 12th on Amazon.com,'s bestseller list in non-fiction. This book received positive reviews from a former CNN producer, Chez Pazienza, even from Dave Barry and Stephen King.

Despite the book being a success Jack Shafer, the reviewer of Slate.com, noted that it received very scanty attention from the conventional mass media, although the largest American newspaper, Tucson Citizen, reviewed the book and gave their review about it. He considered the language, acerbic tone and the way the book has criticized the mainstream media, are the reasons that are responsible for the low attention it received from the media. On the other hand, *It's Not News, It's FARK* was more widely accepted in the broadcast medium, with profiles in Fox News, NPR and G4TV. Curtis' first book was later on released in paperbacks.

Curtis lives in suburban Lexington, Kentucky, U.S, where he has two other businesses. He stays with his wife Heather, and their two sons, Chance and Storm.

CHAD HURLEY, FOUNDER OF YOUTUBE

Chad Meredith Hurley, is well known as the co-founder and former CEO of YouTube.com. Chad was born on January 1, 1977 at Pennsylvania. YouTube is one of the world's most popular video sharing website. Chad was born in the family of Don and Joann Hurley and was their second child. He was brought up near Birdsboro, Pennsylvania. He also has one older sister, Heather and a younger brother named Brent. Chad had serious interests in arts since childhood and had grown special interest in computers when he was in high school.

Chad was also an athlete during his school days and was an excellent runner. He was a member of the cross-country program at Twin Valley High School. His school won two PIAA State titles in 1992 and 1994 when he was the member of the team. He also joined Technology Student Association while he was doing his high school. In 1995, he passed Twin Valley High School at Elverson and entered in Indiana University of Pennsylvania for where he completed his B.A. in Fine Arts in 1999. Business 2.0 voted him the 28th person on "50 People Who Matter Now" list in June 2006. Chad Hurley with his partner Steve Chen developed YouTube which they sold it to Google in October 2006, for $1.65 billion.

Chad Hurley also worked at PayPal for eBay before creating YouTube. His work there was to design the logo of PayPal. At PayPal, his colleagues were Steve Chen and Jawed Karim with whom he completed the task. Tagging and video sharing concept of YouTube were also derived by Hurley.

Hurley got to learn about PayPal when he was doing graduation in college. Hurley applied for a job in PayPal and sent his resume and got a call for interview. PayPal was established in California. At PayPal, he was given a task of designing a PayPal logo during his skill testing. The logo he created was so impressive that PayPal used it as an official PayPal logo for several years. At PayPal, he also met Steve Chen and Jawed Karim. They all conceptualized different business and discussed their potential and possibility extensively. PayPal was bought by eBay in an estimated amount of $1.54 billion. At that time, Hurley got a decent amount of remuneration which enabled him to put that money on his future developments. Former chief financial officer of PayPal, Roelof Botha, also proved helpful in their ventures.

Google acquired YouTube on October 16, 2006, for $1.65 billion. According to Wall Street Journal, Chad Hurley had total $345.6 million share out of $1.65 billion deal sale with a closing stock price of $407.01 on February 7, 2007. Hurley became the owner of total 694,087 Google shares given to him directly as well as 41,232 shares were given to his trust. His colleagues and co-founders of YouTube Steve Chen and Jawed Karim got 625,366 shares and 137,443 shares respectively, which were valued at $326.2 million and $64.6 million. This information was given by Google on Feb. 7, 2007, while submitting registration statement to file SEC, according to the journal.

Hurley remained the CEO of YouTube till October 2010, when he stepped down and Salar Kamangar replaced as the new CEO of YouTube, though Hurley still stayed as an advisor for Salar Kamangar.

Chad also invested in a new F1 entrant of 2010 named Team US F1, though team was unofficially closed on March 2, 2010, and the team personnel were also terminated though there was no official word from the owners Hurley, team principal Ken Anderson, or sporting director Peter Windsor as why the team did not compete the race. It is also reported that Hurley is still trying to create some equations to work from F1 through other F1 teams.

Hurley is married to Kathy Clark who is the daughter of Jim Clark, a well-known Silicon Valley entrepreneur. Hurley has two children from Kathy.

Chad Hurley along with his PayPal colleague Steve Chen and Jawed Karim founded YouTube, a video-sharing website, in February 2005. YouTube is a site on which users can upload, share and view videos.

YouTube is now situated in San Bruno, California. Company uses HTML and adobe flash video to show videos of wide variety that are uploaded by its users. Videos may contain interviews, product demonstrations, music videos, movie clips, amateur video blogging, and real life videos, etc. Videos uploaded on YouTube are mostly done by individual users. YouTube is also running a YouTube partnership program in which several organization show their material via YouTube, such organizations are BBC< CBS, Hulu, and Vevo, etc.

Only registered users can post their videos on the site and there is no limitation on any user to post videos while unregistered users can only watch the videos. Registered users can also watch potentially offensive or videos consisting adult content if they are 18 or over 18 years of age.

Founders of YouTube are Chad Hurley, Steve Chen, and Jawed Karim and all three were working at PayPal when they developed YouTube. While Hurley had studied at Indiana University of Pennsylvania, Chen and Karim were classmates and studied computer science at the University of Illinois at Urbana-Champaign.

There has been an interesting story behind the advent of YouTube, though no one is sure how true it is. It is learnt that Hurley and Chen thought about the idea of YouTube while attending a party. They had taken a few videos of that party which they were trying to show them to Jawed Karim, but found it difficult to do so. Karim did not believe that the part happened. At that time, they thought about an application on which people can share videos during early 2005. Hurley later said that, "The idea that YouTube was founded after a dinner party was probably very strengthened by marketing ideas around creating a story that was very digestible".

YouTube was started on investment of $11.5 million, which was done by Sequoia Capital in between November 2005 and April 2006, as a venture-funded technology startup. At that time, they established the head quarter of YouTube above a pizzeria and Japanese restaurant in San Mateo, California. On February 14, 2005, the www.youtube.com domain name was activated and then they developed the website of YouTube in the following months.

The first video of YouTube video was, uploaded on April 23, 2005, of Jawed Karim showing him at San Diego Zoo, titled as "Me at the zoo" and still can be seen on YouTube site.

Initially, in May 2005, YouTube uploaded a beta site for testing the site's characteristics, before its official launch six months later in November 2005. YouTube progressed at a very faster rate since its inception and company stated that more than 65,000 new videos are being uploaded daily on youtube.com by July 2006. According to officials, the site was also attracting 100 million video views every day. In May 2010, ComScore, a market research company reported that YouTube is one of the most popular online video platform in US with 43% market shares and 14 billion video visits. According to YouTube, there are more than 48 hours of new videos that are being uploaded by the users on the site every minute, and in addition, three-quarters of those videos are uploaded from outside US. According to a research, the total bandwidth acquired by YouTube in 2007 is equal to what entire was taking in 2000. YouTube was also ranked number three of the most visit site on Internet by Alexa and only Google and Facebook are ahead of it.

There was a lawsuit filed against YouTube in November 2006 by Universal Tube & Rollform Equipment organization as they also had a similar-pronounced website named www.utube.com, though later Universal Tube changed their site's name to www.utubeonline.com. Acquisition of YouTube was finalized on November 13, 2006.

Though the details about the cost of running and the revenue generated by the site is not provided by Google, but in 2008, Forbes Magazine reported that YouTube had estimated revenue of $200 million through advertising.

In November 2008, YouTube started a section for US viewers named "Shows" in an agreement with companies like MGM, Lions Gate Entertainment, and CBS which allowed them to show their films and TV serials to US users combined with advertisements. This step was taken to counter websites like Hulu in US. Hulu shows program from Fox, NBC, Fox, and Disney. A UK version of "Shows" was also launched in November 2009 which offered 4,000 full-length programs uploaded by more than 60 video partners. An online film rental service for US users was also launched in January 2010. The online film rental service offers its users more than 6,000 films to watch. In an interview Chad expressed his feelings about the partnership of Hulu with Fox, he stated that, "They have since opened up Hulu with FOX. We think that that's great. We actually don't think Hulu would have existed if YouTube hadn't came along, that the industry wouldn't have moved in this direction, where easily viewed streams of full-length shows are available to everyone without signing up, ad-supported, so we feel like we've already had a great influence on the industry to move in that direction to make their content available, but they also realize that they're not necessarily competing with us, they're more competing with video on demand, the TiVos of the world, and those traditional business."[13]

YouTube also started streaming of certain content to users for free. One of those events was Indian Premier League and a total of 60 cricket matches were streamed and it was the first worldwide online broadcast of a major sporting event which had free access for users.

YouTube introduced a new website design and interface on March 31, 2010, to simply the use of youtube.com for users and make it more users friendly and make users to spend more time on YouTube site. Shiva Rajaraman, Google product manager, explained that, "We really felt like we needed to step back and remove the clutter." According to reports, as on May 2010, users were viewing more than two billion videos every day on YouTube. The company described this as "nearly double the prime-time audience of all three major US television networks combined." In May 2011, In YouTube blog, it mentioned that the site is getting more than three billion video visits every day.

Hurley made an announcement of stepping down for CEO in October 2010 and will take a role of an advisor to help the new CEP Salar Kamangar who will replace Hurley. James Zen, a YouTube software engineer, wrote that in April 2011, 30 percent of videos were viewed by 99 percent users on YouTube.com.

---

[13]   http://gigaom.com/video/chad-hurley-how-we-did-it/

One of the biggest criticisms that YouTube has taken is inability to comply with copyright laws. YouTube though shows a message on screen in the lines of "Do not upload any TV shows, music videos, music concerts or advertisements without permission, unless they consist entirely of content that you created yourself" whenever a user uploads a video and if they are copyrighted videos, they are removed from the site, but still users continuously upload copyrighted videos on the site. There is no regulatory made by YouTube to upload these videos but if a copyright holder complains than videos can be taken down according to Digital Millennium Copyright Act.

YouTube also has seen several lawsuits regarding copyrighted material uploading on its site. Organizations such as Mediaset, Viacom, and the English Premier League have accused YouTube of not working on this issue to prevent uploading of copyrighted videos. Viacom filed a lawsuit of $1 billion as they had found more than 150,000 unauthorized video clips uploaded on YouTube. According to Viacom, more 1.5 billion people have already watched these video clips. YouTube replied to Viacom and said that "it goes far beyond its legal obligations in assisting content owners to protect their works."

After the lawsuit filed by Viacom, YouTube took some serious steps in this regards in which they have created a system named Video ID. This system crosschecks all the videos uploaded on YouTube by the users with a database which has copyrighted contents which enables YouTube to reduce the violations of copyright laws. The lawsuit filed by Viacom was also dismissed by a US federal Judge, Louis L. Stanton, who said that," Google was protected by provisions of the Digital Millennium Copyright Act." Viacom later made an announcement to appeal against it further.

In July 2008, the court ruled a decision in favor of Viacom that YouTube will provide the database of users and Viacom program watched by those users to analyze user interests. This judgment created a lot of discussion around the world and Electronic Frontier Foundation criticized the discussion saying that, "it is a setback to privacy rights" Users viewing details could be found through their user names and IP addresses. Louis L. Stanton, a US District Court Judge, refused the issues about privacy and called them "speculative."

YouTube also had its fair share of criticism regarding the offensive content uploaded on the site. These videos may contain defamation, pornography, and criminal contents. YouTube offers its users an offer to flag the videos if they violate the terms and conditions of YouTube. Flagged videos are then inspected by YouTube dedicated employees to decide if they are appropriate to list or not. This system has also attracted criticism as the Government of UK expressed its disappointment by saying that it was "unimpressed with YouTube's system for policing its videos, and argued that proactive review of content should be standard practice for sites hosting user-generated content".

In reply, YouTube said that, "We have strict rules on what's allowed, and a system that enables anyone who sees inappropriate content to report it to our 24/7 review team and have it dealt with promptly. We educate our community on the rules and include a direct link from every YouTube page to make this process as easy as possible for our users. Given the volume of content uploaded on our site, we think this is by far the most effective way to make sure that the tiny minority of videos that break the rules come down quickly."

YouTube videos also allow users to post their comments about the videos, but these comments have also been a topic of discussion in the media for their offensive nature and use of abusive language.

Blake Ross & David Hyatt, Founder of Mozilla software

Blake Ross

Blake Ross co-founded Mozilla Firefox with David Hyatt. Blake Aaron Ross who is an American software developer was born in Miami, Florida, on June 12, 1985. Blake Ross is mostly known for his work in Mozilla in developing a web browser called Mozilla Firefox. He started this project in combination with David Hyatt. He developed one more project named Spread Firefox with Asa Dotzler. At that time, Blake Ross was working as a contractor for Mozilla Foundation. He was also nominated for Wired Magazine's top Rave Award in 2005, the name of this award was Renegade of the Year. Ross was also included in the list of Rolling Stone magazine in 2005.

Ross developed his first website when he was a 10 year old kid and began programming as a professional while studying in middle school. He made a huge contribution to open-sourced Netscape. He worked at Netscape Communications Corporation as an intern. He was only age 15 then and was still in high school at Gulliver Preparatory School. Netscape was on a life support when Ross joined the company and its web browser was getting the wadding beat out of the company by Microsoft's Internet Explorer. It had only one thing going its way and that was it was open source software. It works differently; there are no definite numbers who can work on the software. Being an open source anybody can work on it in a voluntary manner and without pay.

Ross along with some of his colleagues decided to start a new version of Netscape in 2002. The version, that would quit all the fancy features of the software and go for stability, simplicity and speed. They named this new browser as Firefox and the rest is history.

In an interview Blake stated that, "When over 30,000 users come to you and say "We want to help you spread the word about this thing," you know you're doing something right. These people come to us because they love their new online experience. Firefox was designed from the ground-up to be easier to use than any other browser on the market. We want to make the web easier for people of all backgrounds. Happier users reduce problems and thus reduce headaches among university and corporate IT departments. Dozens of universities and corporations have already come to us to thank us for the time our product saves them downloading new security patches and cleaning spyware and viruses off users' computers." [14]

Ross graduated in 2003 from the school. In 2003, after passing out from school, he took admission in Stanford University where he is currently studying, but does not attend the classes because of his work and is on leave of absence. Right now, he lives in Mountain View, California.

Ross actually came into limelight when he developed Mozilla Firefox web browser with David Hyatt. Firefox was born while he was interning at Netscape where he was using Netscape web browser which was far from captivating because it had some new codes added by America Online as America Online had purchased the Netscape.

The idea of developing user friendly and easy to use web browser envisioned for there. Ross and Hyatt both started working on developing such kind of a browser through open source project which gained popularity. Mozilla had started working on Firefox and Thunderbird with its full resources by 2003 and Firefox was launched in November 2004. Ross was only 19 year old then. Microsoft's internet explorer was the most popular web browser at that time and the advent of Firefox had an adverse effect on internet explorer's popularity.

In a very short period of time, Firefox had become the first choice web browser for web users and it captured a huge market share very quickly.

---

[14]   http://www.insanely-great.com/news.php?id=3993

According to reports, Firefox had achieved 100 million downloads in less than a year. As per the reports of October 2006, Firefox clocked 2 million downloads in the initial 24 hours and the web surfers switched to Firefox at the rate of 7 million per month.

They displayed an ad on the New York Times related to the product that they created, and got an extensive response to that, when Ross was actually asked about that ad, he stated that, "The New York Times ad kills a number of birds with one very large stone. It serves as a statement to many different groups. It's a statement to the world that Firefox 1.0 has arrived, that it's ready for them to try, that it's not some small fry alternative browser which only advertises on Slashdot. It's a statement to our community that we're proud of their accomplishments and that we want to show off their names to the world. It's a statement to the industry that you don't need an enormous marketing budget and unlimited resources to advertise in people's living rooms; all you need is a solid product, which will lead to a passionate community, and the rest will follow. And finally, it's a statement to the open-source world that open-source software and end-user software are not diametrically opposed, that an open-source program can be directly marketed to over one million NYT readers" [15]

By joining hands with Joe Hewitt, another colleague of his from Netscape who also created Firebug and helped in Firefox interface and code, Ross started a new company called Parakey. It was an interface they developed to fill the distance between the desktop and the web. In IEEE Spectrum issue in November 2006, Ross wrote an article in which he gave all the details about his company and the technical details of the program they are working on. Later, it was reported by BBC that on July 20, 2007, Facebook had acquired Parakey. Ross also wrote "Firefox for Dummies" that was published on January 11, 2006. Ross now works at Facebook as a Director of Product.

Dave Hyatt

David Hyatt is an American software developer who was born on June 28, 1972. He currently works at Apple Inc. since July 15, 2002. At Apple,

---

[15] http://www.insanely-great.com/news.php?id=3993

he works with the team of safari web browser and WebKit framework. When Safari was released with versions 1.0 and beta releases, Hyatt was the member of the team which developed these web browsers. Currently, he works as an architect at Apple for Safari and WebKit software.

Hyatt also worked at Netscape Communications in between 1997 to 2002. At Netscape, he worked on Mozilla Firefox web browser. He also developed software named Camino, which was then known as Chimera while working at Netscape. Hyatt along with Blake Ross worked on Firefox. He designed tabbed browsing for Chimera and Firefox. Hyatt also has a big hand in creating first specification codes for XBL and XUL markup languages.

Hyatt finished as undergraduate from Rice University, and for his graduate program, he went to University of Illinois at Urbana-Champaign. For Shadowrun community, Hyatt developed software called Shadowland Six. This is a forum and discussion server. As a freelance writer, he wrote books like "Renraku Arcology: Shutdown and Brainscan" for Shadowrun. David Hyatt is also a member of the W3C's CSS Working Group. He edited HTML5 draft specification till March 2010, but after that, he resigned from that job.

In 2006, Mike Connor asked Debian to comply with Mozilla standards while using Thunderbird trademark for their redistribution of Thunderbird software. This chaos raised some branding issues, though Mozilla Foundation did not approve the proposed modifications and the name for the software stayed the same.

Mozilla Firefox program and other software developed by Mozilla were re-branded by Debian Project in 2006. As a result, Debian was able to distribute the software with permitted modifications. After this, Debian did not have to fulfill the trademark requirements made by Mozilla Foundation. Debian gave new names to Mozilla software like Mozilla Firefox was changed to Iceweasel; Mozilla Thunderbird was given a name Icedove; and Iceape was given to SeaMonkey. These changes were introduced in the new version of Debian (Etch). Mozilla Sunbird was re-branded as Iceowl and added to unstable branch of Debian in July 2007.

Firefox is a trademark owned by Mozilla Foundation, and according to them, the use of trademark without special permission is not allowed and is illegal. No one can use this trademark for any unofficial build unknown to Mozilla. Firefox name and official logo with Firefox source can only be compiled after the permission from Mozilla. Debian project works in accordance to Debian Free Software Guidelines to distribute the software for free.

Firefox logo does not meet these guidelines which is why it cannot be distributed by Debian with the original trademark and logo. In 2004-2005, Mozilla trademark policy issue had become a subject of a long debate in Debian Project. As a result of this debate, the name "Iceweasel" came out which was used to re-brand Firefox. This name was first suggested by Nathanael Nerode in reply to Eric Dorland who suggested "Icerabbit." Motive behind this was to make a parody of "Firefox." The "Iceweasel" was used for re-branding Mozilla Firefox according to Mozilla Trademark Policy. Iceweasel has become the most common name used for a re-branded Firefox now. "Iceweasel route" is used to refer as a re-branding strategy in web world since January 2005.

Matt Groening revealed how the "ice weasel" innovated and said that Friedrich Nietzsche played a big role in it as Nietzsche wrote "Love is a snowmobile racing across the tundra and then suddenly it flips over, pinning you underneath. At night, the ice weasels come." Mozilla initially had given permission to Debian for using the trademarks and Firefox name, but they could not use the original logo and name because Firefox had a proprietary copyright license which was not compatible with the Debian Free Software Guidelines. So, Debian had started using the substituted name and logo.

It was in February 2006, when Mike Connor from Mozilla Corporation sent a letter to Debian bug tracker informing them that the way they were using the Firefox was not acceptable for Mozilla. He also stated they have decided to rethink about the agreement they had done previously with Debian as the same agreement allowed Debian to use Firefox name.

Furthermore, he also communicated with Debian and explained the new trademark policies. With new policies applied, it had become essential that they could only use Firefox name while also using rest of the branding as well and Mozilla Corporation should approve all the browser changes.

New policy of Mozilla caused an immediate problem for Debian because proprietary license of Firefox was noncompliant to the Debian Free Software Guidelines and because of that Debian could not use the official Firefox logo. All Debian releases based on Mozilla products were frozen now on a long-term basis and they can be released only after security patch applied by Mozilla to check for any new security issue. According to the revised guidelines, to use the Firefox brand name, Debian will need approval from the Mozilla Corporation and would need to have security patches for all the projects. However, Debian stated that giving its security to an outside corporation is not a good idea for the company.

Iceweasel, Icedove, and Iceape names were first used for Debian project's unstable repository on November 20, 2006, on October 14, 2006, and on December 1, 2006, respectively. This fact has been mentioned on qa.debian.org.

On November 11, 2006, Thunderbird was removed and Icedove was taken by Etch. After that, on January 11, 2007, Iceape was migrated to Etch. The old Mozilla suite was removed on October 6, 2006. Firefox was also removed when Iceweasel migrated on January 18, 2007. Debian 4.0 (Etch) was Debian's first stable release which included Iceweasel, Icedove, and Iceape and was released on April 8, 2007. Ricardo Fernandez Fuentes drawn new logos for Debian to fit their new names and the old unbranded Mozilla logos were replaced by them. Debian's new projects were designed for Linux and GNU.

However, all the four applications of Debian such as Iceweasel, Icedove, Iceowl, and Iceape are derived concepts of Firefox, Thunderbird, Sunbird, and SeaMonkey, owned by Mozilla Corporation, but still some Internet-based services from Mozilla, such as Mozilla plugin finder service and Mozilla add-ons and their update notifications will still be used by these re-branded products of Debian. The use of non-free components, such as Flash, though did not undergo any changes.

Icedove is an e-mail application which is distributed by the project. Mozilla Thunderbird is the actual platform on which it has been based and made completely as free software. Icedove provides a free version of the Mozilla Thunderbird e-mail client. Icedove does not have proprietary artwork and plug-in repositories of Mozilla Corporation as these are non-free free software.

Debian Project also distributed Iceape which is an Internet suite. Iceape is a SeaMonkey concept and is also made as free software. Their aim is to provide an option for Mozilla SeaMoneky which also is an Internet suite, and Iceape is also kept in synchronization with upstream development of SeaMonkey. Similarly, Iceape also does not have non-free proprietary artwork and plug-in repositories of SeaMonkey, very much like Icedove.

Later Debian launched Lenny, another internet suite which was made to replace Iceape because of lack of development support within the Debian community. Iceape libraries like iceape-dev and iceape-dev-bin can still be accessed, but the software has been removed. However, a newer version of Iceape was later added with Lenny, which included the current stable, squeeze. It was the launch of Seamonkey 2 that prompted Debian to make a new version of Iceape.

Based on Mozilla Sunbird, Debian created Iceowl which is a calendar application and is also distributed as free software.

Matt Mullenweg, Founder of WordPress

Matthew Charles Mullenweg was born in Houston, Texas on January 11, 1984. He is an entrepreneur who lives in San Francisco, California. He developed and founded one of the most popular open-source blogging software WordPress. He also writes his own blog ma.tt on a hacked domain. He used to work at CNET but left the job to work on various open source projects. He is also known as a speaker at conferences like Northern Voice in Canada and at WordCamp events.

Automattic is the business behind WordPress.com as well as Akismet which he founded in 2005. Mullenweg completed his High School in Performing and Visual Arts and learnt jazz saxophone. Mullenweg also uses Dvorak Keyboard.

When Matt went on a trip to Washington D.C., where he participated in the National Fed Challenge, he started using b2/cafelog blogging software to manage the photos he was taking on the trip. He also wrote some codes on typographic entities and cleaner permalinks.

Matt Mullenweg wrote on his blog, that he is planning of forking the software to make it up to date in regards to its web standard and his needs, in January 2003, several months after he had stopped the development of b2. Soon after that, Mike Little contacted Mullenweg and together they started a new blog service called WordPress by using b2 codebase. The original developer of B2, Michel Valdrighi, soon joined them in their venture. When they started this, Mullenweg was fresher at the University of Houston and was only nineteen years old.

Next year, in 2004, he founded a Global Multimedia Protocols Group in company of Eric Meyer and Tantek Çelik. Their group GMPG created first Micro formats.

His colleague at WordPress, developer Dougal Campbell and he joined together and launched Ping-O-Matic in 2004. Ping-O-Matic is made to notify search engines like blog updates for Technorati. Right now, Ping-O-Matic manages more than 1 million pings per day. A radical price change of WordPress Movable Type in May 2004 lead word press users to go for alternative options, and according to some reports, this event was called the tipping point for WordPress at that time.

He started working for CNET in October 2004 where he worked on WordPress for CNET and helped them with blogs and new media applications. Later next month, he moved to Houston, Texas and dropped out of college. Mullenweg made another announcement in December 2004 about his new project called bbPress. He wrote bbPress from scratch during holidays. In February 2005, WordPress team released a new version WordPress 1.5 "Strayhorn." This version of WordPress achieved over 900,000 downloads. With this launch, they introduced some new features in WordPress such as theme system, moderation features, and also redesign the front and back end.

In an incident in early April 2005, there were 168,000 hidden articles that were found by Andrew Baio on WordPress. These articles were using cloaking technique for advertising which Mullenweg accepted that it was questionable and he then removed all those articles from the website.

Though he stayed quiet for a year after that, but he then announced in October 2005 that he is going to leave CNET to concentrate on the development of WordPress completely.

Akismet too was launched publically on October 25, 2005. Akismet was made opened in an effort to stop comment and trackback spamming. The method was to use collected inputs from the people who are using this service.

By November 2005, WordPress.com no more stayed an invite site only and was opened for everyone. A company named Automattic was announced on December 2005 to take WordPress and Akismet ahead. This company employed developers who worked on WordPress and contributed significantly to the development of WordPress, one of them Ryan Boren became the lead developer for the company. Other than him, Donncha O Caoimh who created WordPress MU was also appointed. At the same time, a deal was finalized with Yahoo! Small Business web hosting regarding the license and development of Akismet and WordPress. In January 2006, a former Oddpost CEO and Yahoo! executive Toni Schneider joined the Automattic as CEO. The member count of Automattic had gone up to 5 with the appointment of Toni Schneider.

Polaris Ventures, True Ventures, Radar Partners, and CNET invested around $1.1 million in Automattic in April 2006 through a Regulation D filing. This news was confirmed by Matt Mullenweg, himself, on his blog. They organized their first WordCamp conference in July 2006, and they made it possible only in three days. The conference was organized in BarCamp style. More than 300 people attended the event at Swedish-American Hall in San Francisco. On October 31, 2007, they held their first WordCamp out of US in the capital of Argentina, Buenos Aires. Matt Mullenweg was honored by PC World in March 2007, as #16 of the 50 Most Important People on the Web. At the age of 23, he was the youngest member to achieve this feat at that time.

Mullenweg bought Gravatar service in October 2007 and was also reportedly offered US$200 million for his company Automattic, but he refused to sell the company. In January 2008, a total sum of US$29.5 million was invested by Polaris Venture Partners, True Ventures, Radar Partners, and the New York Times Company in Automattic. Mullenweg on his blog revealed that the investment came after he refused offers to sell the company and decided to keep it intact and independent. This assured investors and prompted them to provide funds to the company later. Automattic had increased to total 18 employees at that time.

Linux Journal published a picture of Mullenweg in July 2008 wearing a Fight Club t-shirt. He was also put on the cover of business section by San

Francisco Chronicle later that month. Alexa ranked WordPress.com at #31 with more than 90 million page views monthly.

Press coverage for Mullenweg was continuously increasing. One more article came in September 2008 in which Inc. Magazine rated him in top Entrepreneurs aged U-30 in US. He was also rated one of the 25 Most Influential People on the Web by BusinessWeek.

Mullenweg was named an honorary patron of the University of Philosophical Society in 2009 for his contributions to information technology and culture. His company Automattic had increased its employee numbers to 35 by January 2009 and at that time, in an interview given to USA Today, he said that his company is growing in stature with profits, established an office on Pier 38 in San Francisco, and have also gotten a client in CNN for WordPress.com.

WordPress offers a quite a few features to the users and consists of web template system which is made by using a template processor. Widgets can be rearranged without editing PHP or HTML codes. Users can also install and switch between different themes. Advanced customization could be done by editing PHP and HTML codes available in themes. One of the best features of WordPress is an integrated link management which is search engine friendly and has a clean permalink structure. It is also able to assign nested, can derive multiple articles categories, and also supports tagging for posts and articles. Automatic filters provide options of standardized formatting and help styling of text in articles. WordPress also displays links to other sites that are linked to a post or article and follows Trackback and Pingback standards. WordPress also has a rich plug-in architecture which enables users and developers to add new features and extend functions in their WordPress blogs other than the default installations available.

In the supervision and guidance of Matt Mullenweg, WordPress has already collected quite a few awards in its stable, such as a Packt Open Source CMS Award in 2007. the best Open Source CMS Award in 2009, the Hall of Fame CMS category in the 2010 Open Source Awards, the Open Source Web App of the Year Award at The Critters in 2011.

On July 10, 2007, they held a discussion on WordPress ideas forum where Mark Ghosh wrote a post on his blog "Weblog Tools Collection," after which Matt Mullenweg decided that the theme directory of WordPress will not host the themes that contain sponsored links. However, sponsored theme users and designers criticized WrodPress for this move. On the other hand, many other users who consider these kinds of themes as spams applauded this brave decision by Mullenweg. Shortly after that, WordPress theme directory was ceased and it declined accepting any new themes whether they had sponsored links or not.

Though on July 18, 2008, WordPress added a new theme directory which was developed like a plug-ins directory and it had an automated program to examine themes uploaded on it as a first step filter. As a second step for themes filtering, all the themes will go under the eyes of a selected person appointed to do this job.

WordPress removed over 200 themes from the WordPress theme directory on December 12, 2008, due to the non-compliance with GPL License requirements.

Matt Mullenweg, after releasing WordPress version 3.0, wrote on his WordPress blog that process of releasing new WordPress software is now abandoned for a while to concentrate more on expansion and improvement of the WordPress community. WordPress 3.1 was released in February, 2011, after a long aperture and 3.2 is supposed to be released in the first half of 2011. The minimum requirement for PHP and MySQL versions will also be increased after the launch of WordPress 3.2 version.

WordPress had also encountered several security issues in the softer releases which were vulnerable to attacks and hacks. In an event, it was reported that WordPress software had several uncovered security issues in 2007 and 2008. In a report came out from Secunia, it was mentioned that they had found 7 un-patched security advisories out of total 32 in April 2009. Most of these un-patched security issues were given rating of "Less Critical." Secunia claims that they have a complete list of vulnerabilities found in WordPress.

In January 2007, an attacker developed an exploitable code called back door by making the full use of the vulnerabilities found in one of the project site's web servers of WordPress. Through this code, many high profile search engine optimization blogs including some low-profile commercial blogs were attacked on downloading of WordPress 2.1.1. Therefore, WordPress took an immediate step and released WordPress 2.1.2 after rectifying the issue and users were also advised to upgrade it with the immediate effect to avoid further discrimination.

According to a study in May 2007, 98% of WordPress blogs were exploitable by hackers because most of them were still running outdated and unsupported versions. The founder of the PHP Security Response Team, Stefan Esser, talked about the security deficiencies of WordPress. This was an interview that happened in June 2007 where he also mentioned that there are critical problems in software architecture of the WordPress due to which it is not able to cite and prevent the problems at the earliest. The criticality of these applications also made it difficult to write coding of SQL injection programs for security.

With time, WordPress made their securities more fool proof and their new versions are more secured with very minimal security issues. The latest critical security issue, worth mention, was found on WordPress 2.7 which was released in 2008. Security plug-ins of WordPress can be used for individual installations.

Initially, WordPress was limited to one blog per installation, although users could use multiple concurrent copies and could run them from different directories if they are designed to use separate database tables. Advent of WordPress 3.0 made multiple blogs possible for the users by using WordPress Multi-User fork of WordPress which was developed to enable users to create multiple blogs within one installation and these blogs will be managed and monitored by a centralized maintainer. This development also called WordPress MU or WPMU. The users who had website could create their own blogging community and were able to control it from a single dashboard by using WordPress MU. For each blog, WordPress MU adds eight new data tables.

Matt Mullenweg and Mike Little had co-founded WordPress project. The core developers involved with the project are Ryan Boren, Peter Westwood, Matt Mullenweg, Mark Jaquith, and Andrew Ozz.

A community called WP testers which is volunteer group has also helped in development of WordPress. These volunteers get early access to nightly builds, beta versions, and release candidates. They can document the errors in a special mailing list or in the project's Trac tool.

Though WordPress had huge contribution of its community in its development, but still it is a distinct part of Automattic, a company founded by Matt Mullenweg. Furthermore, WordPress foundation was made which acquired all WordPress trademarks. WordPress Foundation is an umbrella organization which supports WordPress.org, bbPress and BuddyPress.

WordPress also organizes gathering events for its users and developers which are categorized as informal non-conferences and also formal conferences. These WordPress events are called "WordCamp." They have been organizing these events since 2006 when 500 people attended the first event of WordCamp. Second camp was again held in San Francisco in July 2007 with 400 attendees. In September 2007, another WordCamp was held in Beijing, China, which was the first camp organized outside San Francisco. More than 150 WordCamps have been organized by WordPress till date, but San Francisco WordCamp event is still an official annual conference of WordPress developers and users.

In May 2009, WrodPress was blocked by China's Golden Shield Project because of Chinese Censorship rule which Mullenweg did not think was logical to comply.

Mullenweg's personality and vision can be adjudged by an interview in which he said that his goal always was to earn money by becoming a commercial Robin Hood. His philosophy was very clear and for that, he started developing web services. To achieve his goals, he left his job at CNET and developed a project called Akismet and it worked like a plugin for WordPress. Akismet was a service made to adapt to new kinds of spams and Akismet worked as a spam plug-in and still was able maintain a high level of effectiveness with new spamming practices for a long period of time.

The kind of thought process he had, is now called "Freemium." It means the free services for personal usage and paid services for business purposes and for that, was given a name "Commercial Robin Hood." With this strategy, the company was able to earn profits and still maintain a great relation with users.

His second web service was WordPress.com which has become a huge success in a few years after its launch. It attracts over 200 million visitors per month now days. WordPress.com was established with following philosophy "Well, there's the WordPress software. What would happen if we make it available to a really wide array of people, with the push of a button?" WordPress generated revenue by selling domain names to users, extra bandwidth, and hard drive storage, etc.

In the same interview he said, "I've never been shy about promoting things that I think are better. So a lot of early WordPress users came through personal evangelism, from me talking to people one by one, getting them to switch over. I read a ton of blogs, so it was not random people. It was people who I admired and followed and often had some sort of online relationship with. I was a commentator on their blogs or vice-versa."

He said that he always believed in his projects and works because he knew he is doing right and he is sure about their successes.

SABEER BHATIA, FOUNDER OF HOTMAIL, SABSEBOLO.COM

Sabeer Bhatia, an Indian American entrepreneur who co-founded the Hotmail email service was born to a Punjabi Hindu family in Chandigarh in 1968. His father, Baldev Bhatia worked as an officer in the Indian Army and later as an Indian Defense Ministry personal and his mother, Daman Bhatia was an official at the Central Bank of India.

Sabeer Bhatia had his schooling at Bishop Cotton's School in Pune and later on at St Joseph's College in Bangalore. After passing out from school he joined Birla Institute of Technology and Science (BITS) in Pilani and later transferred to the California Institute of Technology (Caltech) after two years at BITS, and completed his graduation from Caltech. Sabeer joined Stanford University in 1989 to pursue his M.S. in Electrical Engineering. As part of his M.S project work he worked on Ultra Low Power VLSI Design.

Sabeer was always inspired by entrepreneurs such as Steve Jobs and Scott McNealy. Although he was supposed to pursue a Ph.D. degree after his Masters but he decided to join Apple Computers. After serving few years he joined a startup company called Firepower Systems Inc where he worked on a new concept on internet with Jack Smith for two years. They developed a very interesting concept of a web-based database. While working on this idea, they realized the potential of a web based email system and decided to create one called HoTMaiL. It was called "Javasoft", a way of using the Web to create a personal database where surfers could keep schedules, to-do lists, family photos and so on. Thus Sabir co-founded Hotmail

Corporation along with Jack Smith, a colleague at Apple Computers. The uppercase letters in word HoTMaiL spells out as HTML.

HTML is the language protocol used to write a webpage called "Hypertext Markup Language". HoTMaiL, the email service was launched on 4th July, 1996. They decided to provide the service free to the users and generate the revenue through advertising on the website. It was so revolutionary that within six months, the email service HoTMaiL engrossed over four million subscribers. Looking at popularity of the website, Microsoft offered sum of $ 700 million and bought HoTMail on December 30, 1997.

After selling Hotmail, Sabeer Bhatia worked at Microsoft for about a year, and then left the company to start another website, Arzoo Inc. which was shut down when the dot-com industry went into recession. Arzoo.com was launched again in 2010 as a travel portal. Sabeer also started another website "BlogEverywhere" to capitalize on the emerging blogs in the internet. In 2006, he became an investor for NeoAccel, a network security vendor and maker of SSL VPN-Plus.

In November 2007, he released an online office alternative to Microsoft Office called Live Documents. This application allows users to use their documents both offline and online, edit, collaborate and share documents in real-time with others and sync documents between various computers and users. Users can also download their Microsoft Office plug-in which allows them to get the best of offline and online offices suites along with full compatibility for all office document formats. He has also pushed for enabling access to the internet through cable television in Indian homes.

Sabeer launched a free web-based teleconferencing system SabSeBolo.com in 2008. "Sab Se Bolo" a Hindi word means "Let's talk to everyone". His future plans include the development of a new city in India called Nanocity. The aim of this is to replicate the vibrancy and eco-system of innovation found in the Silicon Valley.

Sabeer Bhatia has won several honors and awards. He was awarded as "Entrepreneur of the Year" in 1997 by the venture capital firm Draper Fisher Jurvetson. He was also awarded "TR100" award from MIT to 100 young innovators who are expected to have the greatest impact on technology in the next few years. He was named by TIME as one of the "People to Watch" in International Business in 2002.

In 2008, Sabeer tied the knot with Tania Sharma. Tania is Director of a Pharmaceutical company.

Sabeer is a person who believes that "The biggest risk in life is not to take any risk at all". He was 27 when he decided he was not going to work for others. He believes that he can make much more money by working for himself than working for others.

CHRISTOPHER POOLE
FOUNDER OF 4CHAN

Christopher Poole, born on February 4, 1990, is an American Internet entrepreneur. He is the founder of the websites 4chan and Canvas. 4chan is a unique, image-based bulletin board. Poole originally started this website 4chan under the pseudonym 'moot' (all in lower case). Since its commencement, 4chan has grown in leaps and bounds from a niche site which mainly targeted anime fans, to the one it is now, one of the biggest and the most influential sites on the internet. The site is commanding more than 9 million users in a month, the phenomenon and means to get started on 4chan and to watch and enjoy many admired viral videos.

There was a huge bewilderment about the real identity of moot. Everybody wanted to know what his real name is or what his real identity is. There were various kinds of anticipation regarding the real identity of 'moot'. Some of them even considered him to be hoax, just like his website. He even attended and spoken at several conferences being moot. He has spoken at Massachusetts Institute of Technology and Yale University as being moot.

He never wanted to reveal his real identity as Christopher Poole. He told Lev Grossman of Time, "my personal private life is very separate from my Internet life . . . There's a firewall in between."[16] The real identity of 'moot' as—Christopher Poole was first identified and revealed by The Wall Street Journal on July 9, 2008. On the same day, Time published an interview explaining moot's influence as an administrator who although being non-visible or unknown, has brought about one of the most significant evolution in the field of content collaboration.

---

[16]   http://www.time.com/time/magazine/article/0,9171,1821656,00.html

Grossman began his article by confessing that even he didn't know his real name. But after conducting the interview, he was quite shocked, as moot was a normal 20 year old, lean looking boy who is not much different from others in the age group. moot was selected as one of the "TIME 100": an annual list of "The World's Most Influential People," by TIME Magazine's editors in the Builders & Titans category in the year 2009.

In an online poll carried out on TIME.com, moot was voted as "The World's Most Influential Person of 2008" by the readers. But the results of the voting was questioned, as manual ballot stuffing and automated voting programs were used to influence the voting system. In TED 2010 conference, held in Long Beach, California, he was featured as a speaker in the same year.

According to the reports by The Washington Post, Poole has attended the Virginia Commonwealth University, for few semesters, before he dropped out. It was also reported that he lived with his mother as he was in a lookout for means to earn from his website 4chan. moot held a session at the Paraflows Symposium in Vienna, Austria, on the reason why his website 4chan is reputed as "Meme Factory" on September 12, 2009. In the conference, which was a part of the Paraflows 09 festival, based on the theme of Urban Hacking, moot mainly considered the reason behind such reputation of the site being the anonymous system, as well as due to the lack of data retention, as there is no memory of the site.

At the TED2010 conference in Long Beach, California, which was held on February 10, 2010, moot spoke about the increasing and continued dominance of user identities and sharing of personal details on social networking sites like Twitter and Facebook. He also had a talk about the worth of posting links on such anonymous sites like 4chan. After witnessing the increasing prevalence of such a site, Fred Leal of the Brazilian newspaper Estadão, said that, "it indicates that something extraordinary is happening . . . [4chan] challenges every Internet convention: it is, alone, the antithesis of Google, social networking sites, and blogs." [17]

---

[17]   http://www.webcitation.org/5pF2y1JjE

The idea of 4chan was inspired by a popular Japanese Futaba Channel ("2chan") imageboard. The websites' imageboard is mostly similar to that of 2chan. Most of the activities on the website take place on the imageboard and message boards. The website is divided into six categories, Creative, Japanese culture, Adult (18+), Interests, Misc (18+) and others. The subjects that are discussed in the site is mostly related to manga, anime, sport, technology, music, photography, torrents, hentai, travel, physical fitness along with a random board, which random things can be put up. The website originally hosted a board for discussion on a separate domain named as 'world4ch'; however, it was later moved to the sub-domain dis.4chan.org.

According to Los Angeles Times, 4chan is one amongst the most trafficked imageboards. At one point of time, the Alexa ranking of the site was as high as 56, but now it remains in the 700s. 4chan is a free site and never charged any fee for registration from its users. But its financing has time and again been in problem.

4chan does not have any such system of registration, unlike other sites. Therefore, the users can post anonymous links in the website using any nickname or pseudonym. Tripcodes have been provided by moot instead of registration, as an optional form to authenticate a poster's identity. 4chan has a single employee who is a programmer whom Poole met via an online site Tetris. There are other moderators of the site as well but they work on a voluntary basis.

The random board, amongst all other categories, is the most talked about category. It tops the rank with more than 30% of site traffic. The random board, denoted as /b/ has a unique 'no rules' policy due to its uninterrupted posts, however exceptions are certain banned or illegal content such as child pornography. This category of content is most criticized by the internet critics. Internet memes is another section which grabs most of the attention with interesting catchphrases and images which spreads rapidly across the internet.

Poole created a new website "Canvas" in the year 2010. It is reported that he raised some $625,000, to create the website. The website was on air on January 31, 2011. It featured digitally modified images which are clicked and uploaded by the users. The users are required to self identify themselves using the Facebook Connect. In this site users can upload numerous funny and modified pictures or some other photos and share it with their friends through the site.

Poole gave evidence as a government witness in the trial of United States of America v. David Kernell, in April, 2010. Being a witness, moot explained all the terms used in his website from 'lurker', to 'OP' and many other such terms which are being used in his site. He even explained the prosecutor about the nature of the data that he provided to the FBI. As the part of the search warrant, he provided various other internal data of the website, which includes information about the site as well as how different users can be identified in the site uniquely from the audit logs of the website. He explained the entire proceeding of his website to the prosecutor to maintain complete transparency in the workings of the website.

Poole believes in the value of multiple identities, which he explained in an interview, which took place in the year 2010. He also discussed that he supports anonymity which has brought about great changes in the real world and in the world of internet, where diverse and different identities occur in social networking site like Facebook and Twitter.

Poole's website 4chan is very unusual and one of its kind. It's extremely active and large with millions of users. Since the day of inception in the year 2003, 145 million posts have been put up by the visitors with 3.3 million visitor per month and 8.5 million page views a day. 4chan is considered as the 4th largest bulletin board on the internet. Moreover, this site is popular because of its content and anonymous posts. Internet memes like Chocolate Rain, Rickrolling, Pedobear and lolcats have been made popular by 4chan users.

A number of chief news outlets have profiled Christopher, which includes The New York Times, The Wall Street Journal, TIME, CNN, The Washington Post and the BBC. moot has also participated as a panelist at conferences which took place at Yale Universities and MIT and guest lectured at Yale, Duke, and NYU. At present, he is living in the New York City and doing his undergraduate degree in anthropology and sociology.

KEVIN ROSE, FOUNDER OF DIGG

Kevin Rose was born in Redding, California, on February 21, 1977. Kevin Rose is highly regarded for his internet services and is an American Silicon Valley entrepreneur. In his early days, Rose lived in Oregon with his family, but he spent most of his childhood in Las Vegas, Nevada. He served Boy Scouts of America as an Eagle Scout. In 1992, Rose enrolled at Vo-Tech High School in Las Vegas and then took admission at the University of Nevada Las Vegas to purse a major degree in computer science. In 1998, he dropped out from the university.

Through CMGI, he then worked for a couple of dot-com startups. Kevin Rose has already founded 4 companies called Digg, (which is his most popular venture till date), along with Revision3, Pownce, and Milk, all in partnerships with his colleagues.

TechTV hired Rose as a production assistant for a program called "The Screen Savers." He also co-hosted it for some time. He had his first appearance on TV in "Dark Tip" segments. He also worked on Unscrewed with Martin Sargent. In that show, he provided information about development of computer technology and its activities.

When Leo Laporte left TechTV on March 31, 2004, he took the responsibility of co-hosting the show for them. Comcast's G4 gaming channel merged with TechTV on March 25, 2004, after which several employees were eliminated from the job at TechTV. Rose went to Los Angeles and stayed with G4 for a while until he too was laid off on May 22, 2005. He then went on to start Revision3 and produced podcasts.

First podcasting came out from Rose was the first episode of "The Broken" which released on July 24, 2003; at that time, he was still working on "The Screen Savers" at TechTV.

Kevin Rose, Owen Byrne, Ron Gorodetzky, and Jay Adelson started Digg in 2004. Digg was a technology news website which was launched on December 5, 2004. Rose co-founded Revision3 with Jay Adelson and David Prager in April 2005 in Los Angeles, California. Rose and Alex Albrecht began the weekly podcast on July 1, 2005, named "Diggnation." This podcast included the top stories submitted by Digg users.

Rose launched Pownce, a micro-blogging site, on June 27, 2007. However, Pownce was closed down within one year only. Matt Williams, former general manager of consumer payments at Amazon, replaced Rose as CEO of Digg on September 1, 2010. Later, Rose also resigned from his position at Digg on March 18, 2011.

The fourth company of Rose, 'Milk', became a topic of discussion in technology news world in April 2011. In technology blog TechCrunch, which also reported about the funding of Milk, reporter Sarah Lacy wrote about Milk as "a development lab for mobile Web ideas." She further wrote that Milk team is "going to set out to solve a handful of big old-industry problems using the mobile Internet."

Rose also tried his hand in investing in different companies such as OMGPOP, Gowalla, Twitter, Formspring, Foursquare, Chomp, Facebook, Dailybooth, Square, 3crowd, NGMOCO, and SimpleGeo.

Rose also made a guest appearance on the first episode of R&D TV with Alex Albrecht, co-host of Diggnation. Rose also participated as a contestant on a game show of NewTeeVee Live on November 14, 2007. In these years, Rose had become highly well-known personality on TV and technology world and he and his fellow "Diggnation" host, Alex Albrecht, were also invited as guest on "Late Night with Jimmy Fallon" on March 11, 2009, and April 16, 2010 respectively.

Rose founded Digg in company of Owen Byrne, Ron Gorodetzky, and Jay Adelson in 2004 as a social news website. Before Digg v4 came out, Digg used to operate in a vote out manner where people would vote the stories up or down. This was called "digging" and "burying." Then Rose created new copycat social networking sites with story submission and voting systems to cash in on the popularity of Digg.

Alexa.com ranked Digg at 143rd on the basis of its website traffic on June 11th, 2011, though it was still behind its highest competitor Reddit. Digg's monthly unique US visits were estimated at about 8.5 million by Quantcast.

Kevin Rose and his colleagues, Owen Byrne, Ron Gorodetzky, and Jay Adelson, actually started Digg just as an experiment in November 2004,. The original design of Digg was designed by Dan Ries and was free of advertisements at that time. Very soon, Digg became popular website in the web world; at that time, Google AdSense was added to the website.

The site was updated to Version 2.0 in July 2005. Some new cool features were added to the new version of Digg such as friends list and new interface that was designed by Silverorange, a web design company buy. With this update Digg also added a function "digging" a story without getting redirected to the success page. The developers of Digg also clarified that they will develop and release an improved and more minimalist design of the site in future.

The improved version Digg 3 was launched on Monday June 26, 2006. This version included separate categories created for different components of the site such as Science, Technology, Videos, Entertainment, World & Business, as well as Gaming.

All these categories were also merged together in a "View All" section. Due to the popularity of Digg and a large number of user traffic on the site, it had started facing plenty of problems which was known to be the "Digg effect" by users. Some people called it site being "dug to death."

However, this problem happened when stories were linked on several bookmarking sites simultaneously. It was difficult to measure and assess the impact of the "digg effect" in these cases. Digg maneuvered its main interface on August 27, 2007, mostly in the profile areas. Compete.com survey stated that the domain "digg.com" registers approximately 236 million visitors annually till 2008.

In 2010, in a program "Bigg Digg Shindigg," Digg CEO, Jay Adelson, revealed that Digg is undergoing a major alteration in terms of design and format, while attending South by Southwest Interactive Conference. Wired magazine also caught an interview with him where he explained that "Every single thing has changed" and "the entire website has been rewritten."

Adelson also explained that the duplication errors will also be eradicated by the new version of Digg. This development will also improve the sites durability by preventing some users, which are called "power users," to dominate the site through their submissions. One more feature of user-oriented personalized was also included in the new version. This enabled user to create a user home page by using their digs which allowed users to create what they are interested in.

The commenting system which "helps fight bad behavior like trolling or group-burying" will also be updated to make more secure. These innovation combined have changed the look the site entirely. In brief, Adelson described the new Digg as, "We've got a new back-end, a new infrastructure layer, a new services layer, new machines, everything." It was also mentioned in a Dig blog post by John Quinn that they will introduce Cassandra, a distributed database system and in turn, will no longer use MySQL.

On April 5, 2010, according to some news Kevin Rose was supposed to become the CEO of Digg again as Jay Adelson resigned from the position. Later, it was confirmed that Kevin Rose was not becoming the CEO again and was in search of a new CEO for Digg after Jay Adelson's decision to quit the company. He decided not to take the position as he wanted to spend time on some other ventures or other things like angel investing.

When v4 of Digg released, it lead to a huge backlash from the users because of the bugs and glitches they experienced on the site. Digg developers were criticized through verbal abuses as well. It was also found that there were a large number of posts were done by Reddit which is a competitor of Digg. After the official Digg v4 update, Matt Van Horn, business development director of Digg, left the company. Matt Williams was appointed as the CEO of Digg on September 1, 2010, replacing Kevin Rose, who was working as an interim CEO after Jay Adelson stepped down.

Some reports claimed that Digg officials have been trying to sell Digg since early 2006. Jay Anderson also talked about it in his blog that he would like to talk to some potential buyers, but still Digg is tagged for sale. In July 2008, potential sale talks with Google came out at an estimated amount of $200 million, though on July 25, 2008, deal was canceled by Google, during the due diligence of the sale. Digg was informed by Google about the cancellation of the deal immediately. After Google's decision, Digg received $28.7 million as third round of funding from Highland Capital Partners.

After Digg got the funding boost from investors, the company decided to move to a bigger office. BusinessWeek published a news On December 2, 2008, according to which "Digg Chief Executive Officer Jay Adelson says the popular news aggregation Web site is no longer for sale, and the focus of the company is to build an independent business that reaches profitability as quickly as possible. That means the four-year-old startup will dial back some of its expansion plans, instead prioritizing projects that generate revenue and profit."[18] BusinessWeek on December 18, 2008, assessed financial statements of the Digg and reported that in the first three quarters of 2008, they lost $ 4 million of revenue.

In May 2009, Facebook and Digg were integrated together giving users an excellent feature to connect their Digg and Facebook accounts together. This connection of Digg and Facebook allowed users to display and share their Digg articles on their Facebook page by using their Digg account. Facebook users can also log into their Digg accounts because of this additional integration by only registering their Facebook account on Digg.

Digg also offers a unique feature called Digg Dialogg. Digg Dialogg allows users to submit their questions which will be asked in an interview with a known personality, taken by a selected reporter.

Digg Bar provided users to access Digg comments and analytics while staying on the page and it also made shortening the urls as much as

---

[18] http://www.businessweek.com/technology/content/dec2008/ tc2008121_004686.htm

possible. Digg bar was released on April 2009, and is located at the top of the home page. On April 5, 2010, controversial DiggBar was eliminated in an official announcement by Rose from the official Digg blog. This feature was removed in the 4th version of the Digg website. The decision was made by Rose after he took over temporarily from Jay Adelson the position of CEO.

API Application Programming Interface of Digg was opened to the public on April 19, 2007, permitting software developers to work on user queries and write and let them improve the tools and applications.

Digg algorithm at present works on user diversity, unlike 2006, when to determine the promotion of content, it highly relied upon on flocking behavior among users. At that time, an O'Reilly writer was blamed for stealing CSS of Digg by an anonymous user in a blog post. This story got a lot of coverage and encouragement from Digg users and nearly 3000 votes really flocked it for the Digg.

Though Digg founders Kevin Rose, Jay Adelson and Daniel Burka asseverated their dissatisfaction about this whole episode of Digg's code found on the sites of Mallett, but Mallet replied that code was stolen by the open source contributors of Digg clone, Pligg, which he was using at that time.

Pligg developers were notified about the issue by Kevin Rose and he admitted about the misunderstanding that occurred about Mallet. Later, Adelson thanked Mallett for clearing the issue. In defense of Mallett, an O'Reilly blogger wrote about the failed conception of Digg's mob. Digg mob failed to assess the theft story and blamed Mallet, though Mallet later clarified that the code was indeed stolen.

Initially, Digg was started with a purpose to give freedom of editing to the users editorial powers back to the masses, although Digg started using secret algorithm in its second version which was devoid of its policy of transparency expected by the users. As a result, top users of Digg started toying with the site. An undercover Digg sting operation story was endorsed for cash to get Supernova17 banned.

A niche 'bury brigade' was formed by another group of users. These activists defended and claimed that they are doing these things in congruence with the desires of Digg users. Digg then hired Anton Kast, a computer scientist, who developed a diversity algorithm in trying to stop the domination of these special interest groups.

Digg users also asked for elimination of shouts features in the website, this decision was made in a townhall that was organized by the Digg users. By 2008, Digg's page rank was increased by Google which affected in improvement of profits by creating startups of Digg. It was reported that single front-page blog story was sold for $ 500 in those days. Digg also gave notices to cease the Usocial and Diggfront but they ignored the warnings. Digg v4 release also created more problems regarding the algorithm.

On May 1, 2007, an article containing the encryption key for the AACS digital rights management protection of HD DVD and Blu-ray Disc was seen on the home page of Digg. However, Digg quickly took an action, consulted its lawyers, and that post from the database as well as banned many users for submitting the secret key. After this move, Digg was accused by users for violation of policy of freedom of speech and for supporting corporate removals were seen by many Digg users as a capitulation to corporate benefits.

Jay Adelson stated that according to the cease and desist letters from the Advanced Access Content System consortium and the Terms of Use of Digg, they were forced to remove the article. The action taken by Digg was although defended by some users, but it stormed a revolution of sorts against Digg which resulted in a huge numbers of articles and comments containing the encryption key were written and posted on Digg.

User responses on those articles were coming in heaps which lead the situation to be called a "digital Boston Tea Party." This term was used by the users in their comments. Due to those responses, Digg reversed its decision effectively stating that "But now, after seeing hundreds of stories and reading thousands of comments, you have made it clear. You would rather see Digg go down fighting than bow down to a bigger company. We hear you, and effective immediately we won't delete stories or comments containing the code and will deal with whatever the consequences might be." [19]

There was a report posted to AlterNet on August 5, 2010, by a progressive blogger called Ole Ole Olson also known as "Novenator." Some liberal articles were continuously buried from the upcoming module of Digg for one year which this blogger mentioned in his report and he even reported the DiggPatriots, a conservative Yahoo! Groups mailing list, along with an associated page on coRank were responsible for all this. The blogger stated that the top members of the mailing list were involved in violation of Digg Terms of Usage by creating "sleeper" accounts as and when their main accounts were banned by the administrators. They were also blamed for banning of seemingly-liberal users through exasperating and false "reporting." This blogger post resulted in elimination of the DiggPatriots list and Digg had an investigation started on this matter as well.

Digg updated to version 4, which was launched on August 25, 2010, but site remained unreachable for weeks following the launch. Digg was criticized by a large number of its users due to the removal of some features like bury, favorites, submissions, upcoming pages, subcategories, and history search in Digg v4. Kevin Rose responded on his blog regarding the complaints and reassured user about restoring these features and algorithms in the upcoming pages. The founder of rival site Reddit, Alexis Ohanian, wrote an open letter to Kevin Rose, talking about Digg v4 and its fulfillment of VC meddling. Alexis Ohanian further said that features from other popular sites were and altered and manipulated into Digg v4 and are provided to these users to "give the power back to the people."

Ian Eure, Former Digg engineer, Ian Eure, explained that though the old features of Digg may not be reverted, but it is still possible to sew them in a new architecture.

August 30, 2010, was declared as the 'quit Digg day' by the disappointed Digg users. Front page was filled with the stories of auto submitting publisher account of Reddit which were kept digging by not so flattened

---

[19]   http://about.digg.com/blog/digg-09-f9-11-02-9d-74-e3-5b-d8-41-56-c5-63-56-88-c0

of users of Digg. All the more, Reddit welcomed the fleeing Digg users and also added the Digg shovel to their logo temporarily.

At that time, Traffic on Digg came down tremendously which was considered as the repercussions of Digg v4 launch, and direct referrals from stories on Digg's front page were also dropped according to the publishers. Concerned CEO, Matt Williams, who had newly joined Digg, wrote on his blog post on October 12, 2010, about reversal of the deleted features on Digg. Other than that, RSS submissions were also banned by Digg. Digg said "The simple act of forcing a manual submission helps to combat spam and ensures that quality content appears on Digg."

Kevin Rose, the former CEO of Digg, left the company on March 18, 2011, and got busy in starting a new startup called "Milk." Milk was established to concentrate on mobile web and is a development lab made to create mobile web solutions. Kevin Rose described milk as an "Incubator." According to the report form TechCrunch, it was said that the strategy taken by Kevin Rose for this startup rather different and unique that most other startups in Silicon Valley.

TechCrunch in an interview of Kevin Rose reported that "Rose expects most of the ideas to fail, but ideally he hopes to see one or two to become viable companies that will have a big impact."

Kevin Rose instated further that "We've been upfront with investors that the lab's companies are going after big ideas, not launching continuous small projects." He said. "There is so much opportunity to disrupt old media and old business." Milk is made to counter the old incubator thinking and it also differs from many old trends running in Silicon Valley. Milk has been started with a small team with only five members, other than Kevin Rose, as coders, designers, and other technicians. Rose insisted that it will be a small team in terms of people numbers and they will try to keep it as minimum as possible. Rose has already conceptualized an elite team which will have less than 10 members.

According to TechCrunch, Kevin is much more confident about his products after working at 3 full startups companies and is now working on a strategy of success. It means only successful ideas will be taken further after a test driving of ideas and time will not wasted on unsuccessful ideas and those ideas will be eliminated.

Rose explained, "People talk about pivoting all the time now, but if something isn't working after four months, we'll just shoot it in the head and start again."

Though, exact details about the Milk have not come out yet, but interested users are already welcomed on their website to sign up and got the benefits such as early access and updates about the company through e-mail, Facebook, or Twitter. It was not very surprising when Kevin Rose announced about Milk only a few days after quitting Digg and with all the experience on his side, he was assured of the upcoming success. He also talks about the confidence he has in his abilities, and by establishing in San Francisco's hipster Mission District, Rose had already taken the first step towards its success.

Richard Johnson, Founder of HotJobs.com

Richard Johnson is known for founding HotJobs.com aka Monster.com. He pursued his graduation from Bucknell University and he became a member of Kapp Sigma while studying at Bucknell. As an illustrious entrepreneur, Richard Johnson started his first company in 1988. Johnson is regarded as one of the first pioneers in Silicon Valley.

In 1996, Johnson launched Hotjobs.com. One of the features in his career has been showing of a 30-second advertisement during the Super Bowl in 1999. He took a high risk to raise $1.5 million by mortgaging his house and assets to make the ad possible. That was a gamble, but there is an old saying that fortune favors the brave, Richard also achieved the desired results, and in a very short span of time, sixth-most recognized Internet brand in the world was HotJobs. Later, it proved real prolific year for Richard Johnson as he announced an IPO of HotJobs, which rose over $ 165 million from public investors.

Revenue growth of HotJobs increased tremendously with each passing year. A company which had total revenue of $4 million in 1998 went up to $20 million in 1999, but the revenue statistics took a huge jump in 2000 and grossed more than $100 million. Company established its distinct identity by 2001 as one of the few profitable dot-com ventures. At the end of 2001, Yahoo acquired HotJobs for $468 million.

Johnson was also appeared on television quite a few times during his tenure as the CEO of HotJobs and also attracted print media frequently for interviews and quotes. Johnson made appearances on a morning and evening news programs of a highly successful TV network. He also attended several business conferences as a speaker.

In 2001, he stepped down from his position of CEO and started working for non-profit boards to serve the community and also contributed on conservation missions.

Richard Johnson currently resides at Wilmington, North Carolina, with his family.

HotJobs, an online venture founded by Richard Johnson, was acquired by Yahoo! in late 2001 until early 2002 and became Yahoo! HotJobs. HotJobs developed as a means to job searching for the people. Concept of HotJobs was to work as an online job search engine, advising the users regarding search for the jobs to apply which suit them best and ensuring that they meet the right result and it was conceptualized and executed brilliantly through HotJobs. The companies and employers also found it easy to choose the right candidates for the job they are offering and they had vast options to choose from. The success instilled a great satisfaction in Richard Johnson who worked hard and took several risks to establish this job seeking machinery.

Though it was handed over to Yahoo! in 2001-2002, it was later owned by the owner of Monster.com, Monster Worldwide, in 2010. Later, HotJobs was closed and merged completely into Monster.com.

Richard Johnson, who founded Hotjobs.com, made company's base at 24 West 40th Street, 12th floor in New York City, just across from Bryant Park. Before this venture, Johnson had founded the RBL Agency with his partner Ben Carroccio and Liz Johnson. The initial of the three made it RBL. It was an employment agency for the people qualified in technological streams.

The website initially was started in 1996 and it was known as RBL Agency. The site was developed into an Online Technical Employment Center (OTEC) in 1999. At that time, it was featuring technical jobs only. OTEC employed Christopher G. Stach II, Earle Ady, and Allen Murabayashi at the start who all designed and coded its first version. Silicon Graphics Indy workstations were used for C application development. Contents were created using Apple Macs. Sun and SGI hardware was used to run the site.

The company was also advertised as Yahoo! site of the week and one could purchase that at $1000. HotJobs took part in first conference of Jupiter Communications in February 1996 at New York Sheraton. Ginna Basinger was working for the Sheraton at the time when Richard Johnson offered her to join HotJobs as first sales person of the company in the same event.

In October 1996, Thomas Chin also joined the company. Chin was studying in Columbia University at that time and he acquired the position of company's chief scientist in a very short period of time. Johnson expanded the company operations in 1997 and a few of RBL recruiters were shifted to the Salesforce. Dimitri Boylan was appointed as the head of the sales and marketing department. Kelly Michaelian & Michael Tjoa opened their first remote sales office on the Labor Day weekend in 1997 in Burlingame, CA. The store was opened by HotJobs & OTEC as a joint venture. Company sales person, Ginna Basinger, was asked to transfer to California, leaving New York office, to manage the office there. Company also appointed Michael Johnson, as its first non-New York employee, to work as an Account Executive in August 1997.

With company progressing rapidly, Johnson felt the need to expand the covered office area, so they established the new bigger office in downtown San Francisco, moving on from Burlingame office, in the summer of 1999. That office remained there until the company was disposed in 2002.

"Softshoe," a private label job board and applicant tracking system, was created by HotJobs in 1997. First client of this product was Lucent Technologies.

HotJobs also started showing jobs related to other field along with technology, like accounting, finance, sales, and marketing in 1997. In October 1997, HotJobs published their first newsletter and at that time, company name was also changed from "HotJobs, Inc" to "HotJobs.com, Ltd", which was suggested by Peter Connors, who joined the company as the first marketing manager.

In 1999, company's step to buy an advertisement during Super Bowl XXXIII in $1.5 million really surprised the advertising world as the total revenue of the company itself were only about $2.5 million, but the decision proved to be a boon for the company attaining huge popularity in the world. They hired McCann-Erickson Detroit for production of the advertisement. Through this advertising program, they got huge amount of publicity and revenue went up to $25 million as a result. Immediately after the commercial was played in Super Bowl, company databases were filled with the requests from users and employers. IBM later used this incident to make a commercial.

Company also brought its IPO in late 1999, and by 2000, company's estimated revenue had gone up to $100 million. As an expansion plan, HotJobs acquired a resume processing company, Resumix, Inc. situated in Sunnyvale, California, and it also entered in the enterprise market by cracking this deal. To take the venture further, Tim Villanueva, a former leading developer at Intuit, was appointed as the Chief Technology Officer of Resumix, while former Chief Architect at BroadVision, Chuck Price was appointed as Senior Vice President of Engineering. However, Allen Murabayashi and Thomas Chin left the company soon after HotJobs expanded the leadership department to develop new venture that was started.

Richard Johnson resigned the company as CEO and President in March 2001, and was replaced by COO Dimitri Boylan as the board agreed up on his name to take those positions.

Through an unsolicited bid, Yahoo! bought the company for $436 million in the year 2002, by overcoming the bids of Monster Worldwide, owners of Monster.com, who were also in line to acquire the HotJobs. Later, in February 2010, it was reported that Yahoo is selling HotJobs in a deal of $225 million to Monster and according to the deal a 3 year profit sharing method was also agreed by Monster.com and in exchange will be promoted on Yahoo websites after the acquisition. However, after the acquisition, the HotJobs users were offered a chance to migrate their information and job postings to a Monster.com account.

Monster.com which acquired HotJobs.com from Yahoo is one of the largest employment websites and is owned and developed by Monster Worldwide, Inc. According to comScore Media Metrics in 2006, Monster.

com was one of the 20 most visited websites and there are 100 million websites existed in the world. Monster.com came out in 1999 as a result of merging of two of the most popular job sites, The Monster Board (TMB) and Online Career Center (OCC). Monster made it easy and possible for users to search jobs according to their location and skills.

A database of more 150 millions resumes and over 1 million job postings have established Monster as the largest job search engine by 2008. Monster is getting more than 63 million seekers every month. Total number of employees working for the company is 5000 who are spread in 36 countries. Monster established its headquarters at Maynard, Massachusetts, United States. However, Indeed.com relegated Monster.com in October, 2010 and became number one job site in USA. Monster.com also developed a Monster Employment Index to keep up with the successful job employment through Monster.com.

The Monster Board was founded by Jeff Taylor who worked as CEO and "Chief Monster" for many years. Jeff Taylor along with Christopher Caldwell from Net Daemons Associates tighter developed this job searching facility with a web browser in an NDA lab on a Sun Microsystems Sparc 5.

TMP launched its IPO in December 1996 and the shares were traded on NASDAQ with a symbol "TMPW." The Recruitment Advertising network, of TMP was expanded in 1998 which enabled it to become one of the largest recruitment advertising agencies in the world.

The Monster Board changed to Monster.com in January 1999 when it merged with another TMPW service called Online Career Center. Bill Warren, the founder of Online Career Center, became the first president of Monster.com after this merger.

Bill Warren in 1997 was awarded with Pericles Pro Meritus Award of Employment Management Association which was presented by EMA/SHRM recognizing his contribution in founding the online recruiting on the Internet.

In 2001, TMP Worldwide was also added to S&P 500 Index. Furthermore, in 2003, they started trading under NASDAQ with new ticker symbol "MNST" as they changed the corporate name from TMP Worldwide to Monster Worldwide, Inc.

Monster.com had also started showing their advertisements on the Super Bowl from 1999 and they regularly played their ads till Super Bowl XXXVIII. The first commercial came out form Monster in Super Bowl 1999 was "When I Grow Up." It was created by Mullen and was asking job seekers, "What did you want to be?" The ad was highly acclaimed and is the only ad to get a place in the "Best Television of 1999" list of Time magazine. Monster bought a URL and trademark named Jobs.com in 2002 for $800,000 million, finding it one of the most desirable URL on the web.

HotJobs offers free services to the users who are seeking hobs and a single user can post up to 10 different resumes. User first needs to sign up on the site which ensures secured browsing of the jobs and employers. Users are also informed about the results through e-mails. Users can also extract the statics regarding how many employers have reviewed their resumes. By using various tools available on the site, users can calculate the estimated salaries, employee stock options, and research plans.

HotJobs also obliges users with an e-mail mentioned a "Job Tip of the Day." There are several other options also available for users work on such as Career Tools tab lists including education center, interviewing advice, and resume building. "HotBlock" option allows users to block specific employers to see their resumes.

Employers also get access to resume search engines where they can view resumes, and also can add new jobs, edit, or delete them at any time without any cost. Employers can track their postings as well can use communication devices such as letter templates and notes.

Yahoo! HotJobs was voted the "Best General Purpose Job Board for Job Seekers" for 2002 and 2003 by job seekers itself. Recruiters' votes made Yahoo! HotJobs the "Most Recruiter-Friendly General Purpose Site" in 2003. This survey was organized by WEDDLE'.

Richard Johnson is also famous as the founder of dot-com wonder HotJobs. com. In BusinessWeek07 held in UNCW, Richard Johnson participated as speaker and he impressed every one with the way he spoke himself out about his desires, philosophy, and way of work. There were several speakers who participated but his story was unique and captivating. He is a man who put everything he had on a SuperBowl advertisement and actually pulled it very well. After that, a piece of article about him was published on internet talking about his qualities and distinct abilities which distinguished him from other standing with him.

The article stated that he could take benefit out from as small a thing as needle. Making publicity from little spats and issues was an easy way to seek the attention of the people. In an incident when his advertisements were rejected by Fox, he converted it into a big issue as to why these rejections are happening which ended giving his organization a huge media coverage. His philosophy was to analyze the negative points and turn them into positives. In his projects, he would try and get as much information as possible and advice he could get and collect it and introspect what is the need for the hour and then work according to that. It made me achieve more things what he could have actually done without it. Decision making was in his hands and he knew what is right for the organization. He never let him hit any ego towards any competitor of him and has always been supportive towards his employees.

Johnson had the eye of a jeweler, who can detect a diamond amongst several stones. He had the ability to choose the best person even from a mob which allowed him to appoint the best person and cut anyone who is not contributing to the production. He created and carried out a professional business environment in his organization. He considered professionalism to be the secret behind every successful enterprise.

He always wanted to generate employment for the young generation, so that they can work actively and bring something new and fresh for the organization. He used to hire young people who were willing to learn and imply their knowledge to innovate something new. The average of his company's employees was about 24 years of age. An experienced fresher can be an asset at times to bring new and fresh ideas to the table. He understood this and applied in his ventures.

Thomas Anderson & Chris DeWolfe
Founders of MySpace.com

Thomas Anderson

Thomas Anderson was born on November 8, 1970. He co-founded Myspace.com in company with Chris DeWolfe. He is a Silicon Valley American entrepreneur who introduced Myspace.com, a social networking website which came into the fore in 2003. Anderson also has a default account in Myspace.com, which means, whenever a user makes an account on Myspace.com he gets a pre-added account with his picture in the friends list as a default friend. Thomas Anderson also held the position of president and a strategic adviser in the company for a long time.

The first page of Myspace.com was created in 2003. He was working in a company owned by Brad Greenspan named eUniverse. At that time, Anderson and a few of his colleagues of that company started programming for Myspace.com and the site started evolving from that point onwards and grew from there. Myspace.com became popular very quickly among US web users. Alexa ranked the website at number 70 out of top 500 sites in USA.

Anderson first started working at Intermix. Intermix is actually a changed name of eUniverse. At Intermix, he developed quite a few profitable internet services. At Intermix, Anderson handled spyware software and spam programs. He also developed innovative selling subscription skin medication which became popular everywhere through "Better than Botox?" commercial.

In an American drama-comedy film named, Funny People, Anderson worked along with stars like Adam Sandler, Leslie Mann, and Seth Rogen.

Right now, Thomas Anderson who is also called as Tom Anderson lives in California.

CHRIS DEWOLFE

Chris DeWolfe is the man who in company of Thomas Anderson founded Myspace.com. He is a widely known US entrepreneur and has been a former CEO at Myspace. DeWolfe holds the account number six of Myspace website.

DeWolfe studied at Lincoln High School situated in Portland, Oregon. He passed graduation in 1988 from the University of Washington. He became a member of Beta Theta Pi Fraternity while studying in the University.

On April 22, 2009, DeWolfe stepped down from the position of CEO in an announcement made by News Corp., but DeWolfe would still be working as a strategic adviser at Myspace. He was shifted to Myspace China to execute to work there. Owen Van Natta, former executive of Facebook, was appointed as a CEO in place of DeWolfe. Many a famous publication houses such as BusinessWeek and Fortune have also published his interview and profile in their editions.

Thomas Anderson and Chris DeWolfe both together founded Myspace and popularized the word "My" among the people. Myspace is a social networking website and the head quarter of Myspace is in Beverly Hills, California. Myspace is now owned by News Corp Digital Media and both offices are set in the same building. News Corporation owns both these ventures.

As the CEO of MySpace.com, DeWolfe was accountable for all aspects of the website's strategic vision as well as the carrying out of its global business ingenuities. Under his observation, MySpace redefined the concept of online social networking, while developing itself into the world's most comprehensive entertainment, lifestyle and communication portal. Along the way, DeWolfe led strategic initiatives that extended the site's reach into a number of vertical categories—such as politics (MySpace Impact), online video (MySpaceTV), news, film and music—and at present a total number of 29 international markets.

In 2006, Myspace was rated as the most popular social networking site in US. It maintained its number one position in 2007 as well, but in 2008, comScore reported that Facebook has replaced Myspace as number one social networking site in US. The rating was given based on unique monthly visitors at the site. By 2009, there were 1,000 employees who were working at Myspace, but 30% of whom were released in June, the same year. Lone revenue statistics of Myspace are not available because all statistics are announced by News Corporation in a whole. In May 2011, total unique visitors from US were estimated at about 19.7 million. This estimation was done by Quantcast.

Under the leadership of DeWolfe, MySpace developed remarkably since its launch in the year 2003, with the average of 300,000 additional users signing up on an everyday basis. By integrating blogs, Web profiles, classified listings, photo galleries, entertainment content, as well as user forums, MySpace has developed a community where users can do everything from planning their weekends to connecting up with their friends along with discovering new music. Above 70 million people in the United States visit the website each month, which creates a user composition which includes politicians, filmmakers, comedians, bands, photographers, and several other people who want to communicate with friends along with planning their social lives.

The exact address of Myspace head quarter is Fox Interactive Media headquarters, 407 North Maple Drive, Beverly Hills, California.

History of Myspace goes as far back as 2002 when Friendster was launched, Anderson was working at eUniverse that time and he along with some employees at eUniverse who had accounts in Friendster liked its features and decided to create a new version out of it. The first Myspace version was developed within just 10 days and was launched in August 2003. Brad Greenspan, owner of eUniverse, kept a close eye on the project and all the development was approved by him. Complete infrastructure was provided by him to developers like hardware, finance, technical help, and human resources. They did not face any problem regarding appropriate server and bandwidth for the project. Project development went smoothly until it was ready to launch. They stayed unaware of any startup problem people usually face. Thomas Anderson, Chris DeWolfe, and Josh Brenan along with a bunch of computer programmers worked extensively to make it a successful program under the roof of eUniverse.

The eUniverse employees were the first people to use Myspace and became its members. A contest between the employees to signup the most users was started by the company. The company held contests to see who could sign up the most users. All the resources of eUniverse were used to advertise Myspace, among 20 million users of eUniverse to give it a kick start in the race of many other social networking websites. A technology expert was appointed by Brad Greenspan who played an important part in stabilizing the Myspace platform.

The domain name MySpace.com was not available and was purchased by YourZ.com. There motive behind the purchase of this domain was to create an online data sharing and storage site. YourZ.com was holding the rights of Myspace and MySpace.com. By 2004, both the sites existed as a brand associated with YourZ.com and from a virtual storage site, it transformed into a social networking site. A friend of Dewolfe had acquired the URL domain MySpace.com who reminded Dewolfe about it that he purchased that URL and was intended to start a web hosting service, but he dropped the idea because of slump in dot-com business. Both Dewolfe and his friend had already worked in virtual data storage business together. By 2004, Myspace that was supposed to become a storage site had transitioned into a social networking site.

Later, Chris Dewolfe also suggested a payment model to apply for Myspace services, a few days after the site was launched, but Brad Greenspan was not much impressed with the idea. Greenspan talked about keeping the site free to use to attract more users. It was not very logical to charge a fee from the users because it would detract the users away, and it can only be successful if we have a huge community of Myspace.

Myspace equity was up for the company employees to purchase including Anderson and DeWolfe till July 2005. News Corporation, owned by Rupert Murdoch, purchased Myspace and eUniverse, now known as Intermix Media, for US$580 millions. News Corporation is a huge brand and organization. It is a media and television group which owns several popular entities in US such as Fox Broadcasting and several other media houses. The total bidding amount was a sum for value of Myspace and eUniverse in unison, but according to the opinion of a financial advisor, the value of Myspace was estimated around US$327 million.

As an expansion plan, News Corporation in January 2006 announced their plans to launch Myspace in UK. The motive behind it was to make their presence felt in UK music scene. The UK version of Myspace was launched later and since then Fox has launched several versions of Myspace in different countries including China.

On August 9, 2006, Myspace hit its 100 million users mark and this user account was created in Netherlands. Though Thomas Anderson have been known as founder of Myspace, but still the status of him being the Myspace founder has always been a disputed topic among the people.

Google was leading an OpenSocial alliance which included some successful social networking sites like Plaxo, LinkedIn, Ning, SixApart, Friendster, and Hi5 and Myspace along with Bebo also joined the alliance later. This alliance created standards for social networking sites in terms of the features and applications for developers.

Though Google had developed their own social networking site named Orkut, but it failed and flattered to deceive the web users in US and it was a huge setback for Google, though Orkut's success in Brazil surprised everyone. However, still Google's presence was enough to keep the balance, to counter Facebook's monopoly among social networking sites as Facebook had refused to join the alliance and kept working independently.

Myspace had become the leading social networking site in late 2007-early 2008 leaving behind Facebook with more visitors than any other social sites. According to some reports in 2007, the total value of Myspace was estimated at $12 billion when News Corporation tried to unite it with Yahoo, though did not succeed.

After so many highs, lows were inevitable and it happened to Myspace too, as it started losing membership. This process started in mid 2008 when Facebook replaced Myspace for number one social networking site in USA. Lack of innovation and reaching saturated state in terms of new developments did not help Myspace. Myspace's strategy of being a music and entertainment centered social site and a portal like feel have also been the reason of its sudden decline.

A complex design with full of advertisement has also been a problem for Myspace and a Myspace executive blames this to a deal with Google for US$900 million which is a long term deal for 3 years and according to the deal, Myspace was forced to show more number of advertisements on the site which has made it very congested-looking site and there was no space left for any new innovative features on the site page and if they minimize the ads, the revenue generation will fall. At this point, Facebook edged Myspace by giving fresh features to users. Because of Myspace's inability to improve with time, a large number of Myspace users, aged 18 to 24, have migrated to Facebook.

According to Alexa ranking came out on April 19, 2008, Facebook edged Myspace in the race of rankings but it was just a start of decline. The lowest point for Myspace came in June 2010, when it was ranked at number 80 while Facebook was sitting happily at the second position.

Jonathan Miller, former AOL executive, took charge of digital media business of News Corporation in early 2009. Miller changed all the equations and combinations of executive team. In this renovation, Tom Anderson, Myspace President, stepped down from his position, while Owen Van Natta, former Facebook COO, replaced Chris DeWolfe as Myspace CEO. Rupert Murdoch, the Chairman and CEO of News Corporation, expressed his disappointments regarding Myspace of not fulfilling his expectations by not reaching $1 billion revenue mark.

Now the new strategy was to develop Myspace as a social entertainment website rather than a social networking website or a competitor to Facebook. They started focusing more on entertainment stuffs like movies, music, and celebrities to mould it into a new genre and a fun site. In their quest to offer something more, Myspace joined hands with Facebook which enabled artists like musicians, singers, and bands to manage their Facebook profile while on Myspace. Mike Jones, Myspace CEO, quoted that "Myspace now is a complementary offer to Facebook Inc., which is not a rival anymore."[20]

In March 2011, comScore published another market research results for website according to which in January and February 2011 about 10 million users left Myspace. Unique user numbers went down from 95 million to 63 millions in that period. Largest reduction in unique visitors was noted in February 2011 at 37.7 million with a fall of 44% in comparison to previous year's calculations. It was also stated that this reduction of user numbers resulted in advertisers' unwillingness to make any long-term deals with Myspace.

According to some media reports, at the dawn of 2011, Myspace will be put on sale and reports proved right in February when the site was decided to be auctioned for $50-200 million. The decline in worth of the site happened due to huge loss in 2009 and 2010. Auction deadline was set till May 31 2011, and by that day, they could not get bids more $100 million.

The redesign phase of Myspace was started in 2007 and several new features were added through 2008. During that time, Myspace touched its highs of becoming leading social networking site in US. Most of the features were change in website layout and its functionality. Home page of Myspace was redesigned and some extra features of applications, status update, and subscription were added which were pretty similar to Facebook's features. Music application of Myspace was redesigned in 2008-2009 to make it look more like an online music store such as iTunes and Rhapsody. The ability to make playlists was added as well.

A recommendation search engine was introduced on March 10, 2010, which helped new users to find their favorite games, music, and videos. This search engine will shows results based on previous searches of the users. With these changes, security of an account also went through some significant changes like who do you want to see your account. It was categorized like Friends only, 18 and older, and every one. Myspace

---

[20] http://online.wsj.com/article/SB10001424052748703576204576226620748953038.html

also planned to go on mobile in 2011 with lots of features like mobile applications for games and also offering game alerts via e-mails. Several micro applications will also be released for the site.

Moreover, color scheme was changed in 2010 when a white theme was applied replacing classic blue. Color change was introduced to make the site look like Facebook. The reason behind it was to get their users back from Facebook again. Site navigation was simplified, which was rather complicated before, to increase the user friendliness of the site. In August 2010, Profile 3.0 was launched with some more home page modifications like new Myspace stream to evolve it somewhat like Facebook. The new simplified interface left more space on the user home page which allowed users to do more creative activities there. Addition of simple template creating application made it easier to control the module for users. Templates can be built without using HTML or CSS coding.

A Fotoflecer application as well as a photos section was added in September 2010. Myspace continued to work on improving the website. Myspace also enabled users to integrate their Myspace activity to their Twitter and Facebook accounts, to attract and show others that they are still on Myspace and to bring users back to Myspace. Myspace Movies option was also added to promote movies and movie related media.

Myspace created international site options for users to use their own language, which was launched in 2006. People could see the contents according to their culture and traditions. Advertisements too were shown based on their habits. Date and time formats were also changed according to local preference.

There were several controversies when Brad Greenspan, former CEO and founder of Intermix media accused the sale of the company for cheating shareholders. Greenspan accused that the company was acquired by News Corp. for a lesser value of $327 million while it could have been valued at $20 billion. Greenspan also had put a lawsuit with these allegations, though financial experts refused to accept the claim of Greenspan and a court judge also dismissed the lawsuit filed to challenge the acquisition.

VSS Mani, Founder of JustDial. com (Worth INR 500 crores, or $1.16 billion)

As the dot-com fascination grown all over the world, we got to see different and innovative developments in the last 15 years. Quite a few ideas delivered a big time and it also created new millionaires. People got used to these services and benefitted hugely with it. It encouraged the developers to continue working on new and out of the box ideas. Same kind of an idea was conceptualized by VSS Mani, CEO of JustDial, in 1994.

As necessity always prompts invention, this was the similar case behind building this venture. With bigger markets and many offers for every product, it could lead to confusion as what to choose from those options available and which will be the best option out of so many other available in the market? JustDial and get the answer. This is the whole story line which prompted Mani to start JustDial. Every solution was available at only a call's distance.

Jamshedpur born Mani brought up in Kolkata where he got his complete education along with his degree of CA. There was another similar kind of service that became popular called "Yellow Pages," but it also has its deficiencies associated with it, as it was not available throughout the day and can only be accessed within particular timeline. First time, Mani thought about this kind of an idea was in 1987-1989 when he also started a company in New Delhi to execute his ambitions, but on those days getting telephone connections would take a long time, it might be few months or even years, so it was not that feasible to imply this concept at that time and later, he dropped the idea, but somewhere inside, he still had the desire to work on something innovative.

So, he took a flight to Mumbai with only 50,000 rupees in his bag and started his struggle. He had enormous ideas to execute, but he was hampered by lack of funds. He then started a matrimonial magazine which proved to be a successful and popular venture. Through this magazine, he could earn enough profit which enabled him to start "JustDial" in 1994 with an aim to provide quality service in a short time period. Information was divided in different categories depending on their genres.

Now JustDial services are being provided through phone calls, internet, and SMS. Revenue is generated through audio advertisements which are played whenever a user calls the company to get some information. As and when the call is received, he will be asked to hold on the line for a while until the call is transferred to the executive. During this time, the advertisement is played which enables company to earn revenue. Within 15 years, since when the company was started with a sum of 50,000, the total assets of the company increased, and now the company is estimated at INR 500 crores, with a turnover of 100 crores per year.

Initially, company had only 100 employees and today, there are 2600 employees, who are working all over India. Company covers 240 cities in the country. JustDial progressed incredibly and also attracted investors like "TIGER GLOBAL," a company based in America, which invested INR 77 crores and also a company from Hong Kong called "SAIF Partners" invested INR 50 crores.

Company services were though first started only through telephone, but they needed to make it fast and wanted to reach wide audience, so it was the best idea to start internet services of JustDial. With the advent of JustDial.com, users could access the services through the website. It has become a very popular information site in India now. Around 80 million calls are registered on the company's telephone numbers every year. Starting internet services through JustDial.com has proved a prolific little step for the company in the right direction. The revenue has increased and popularity has grown in all circles with 75 million users visiting the site every year.

JustDial services have already met a 3 million mark in terms of successful dealings between customers and buyers. Now JustDial is planning to launch their service in USA. With 24x7 services, it will be a one of its kind service in US to get necessary information through a single call.

The development of VSS Mani has set an example in India. He is the perfect example of how a man who comes from a small place made his name in one of the most innovative way. Mani who started working in a directory firm as a sales executive achieved this position through sheer passion towards his work and kept his focus on quality and continued improvements to make it better every day. This company has not only become financially successful venture, but also established Mani as an entrepreneur who has a vision to see into the future and is qualified enough to manage limited resources to its full potential.

Success does not come easy and Mani knew it; that is why even when his first venture named "Ask Me" flopped because of lack of infrastructure and funds at that time, he did not go down and kept working to make it real.

Mani was in Kolkata and was pursing graduation as well as doing CA articleship, but he could not complete his CA exams and had to go for a job because of some family matters. He worked as a sales executive at United Database India, a yellow pages company. It was in 1987 when he joined the company and worked there for 2 years. That was the time when he thought about an innovative idea of starting a service similar to yellow pages through phone lines. With some friends of him, he introduced "Ask Me" in 1989, but his idea and "Ask Me" did not yield expected results then.

As he was from a normal middle class family, he lacked in financial aspect and this kind of an idea needed funds in aplenty. Later, he worked on several businesses to earn money. One was a matrimonial magazine, Wedding Planner, introduced in collaboration with "The Times of India."

The best thing about JustDial is they have one of the easiest numbers to dial and remember, which is 69999999 now and it can be dialed from any part of the country. JustDial.com now has become number one local search engine in India now.

JustDial number to dial from mobile is 08888888881. Mobile revolution in India played a huge role in the progress of JustDial in the last decade. Cheap call rates and a large number of mobile users proved a key for the business, as more and more people were able to say "JustDial".

TOM FULP FOUNDER OF NEWGROUNDS

Thomas Michael "Tom" Fulp was born on April 30, 1978, at Perkasie, Pennsylvania. Fulp is the creator and administrator of the popular website Newgrounds. It is a well known site for sharing Flash files. He is also the co-owner of the video game company, The Behemoth. Fulp is also the co-creator of the Flash game Alien Hominid. This particular game was later ported to consoles. He also created the console game Castle Crashers.

Fulp was brought up in Perkasie, Pennsylvania. He received his education from Pennridge High School. In the year 1996, he graduated from there. Fulp suffered from chronic depression when he was a child. Later on he hinted that it was due to an incestuous relationship with one of his uncles. As a child, he never wanted to go to the school as he had a strict and very authoritarian teacher. When he was in the elementary school, he often used to remain sick because of depression. That was the time when he created violent stories and artworks. During the days of Junior High School, Fulp created a fanzine and named it as "New Ground".

On July 6, 1995, he founded Newgrounds as an American entertainment and social media website. Primarily the site hosts games and Adobe Flash animations. Along with an art portal, the site also features music oriented page. Newgrounds is the oldest Flash portal website, and it is most eminent for its automated submission and rating system. Moreover, it is the first website in the history to produce a completely automated user-generated content system.

Newgrounds has it's headquarter and offices at Glenside, Pennsylvania.

The home page of the site displays recently submitted links which are chosen by the administrator. And those are specially showcased as their most preferred ones. The initial front page icon for the user-submitted flash game was posted on the site with the heading of "Tom and Wade Recommend" on April 21, 2003.

Eventually, Newgrounds received more and more number of quality submissions and the Tom and Wade Recommend section of the page grew from 1 to more and more. In 2009, there were 36 icons at that section on the home page. Categorically, there were 12 icons for games, 12 for Flash animations, 8 for art and 4 for music. The pace at which the site developed also increased and the development could be seen in days. It eventually led to the removal of the "Tom and Wade Recommend" section and became a staple on the front page. It made it easier for the users to find quality posts in the site.

The site launched a home page archive on January 12, 2004, maintaining a month-by-month record of Flash content that was believed to be worth displaying on the Newgrounds home page. This comprises of either those people who performed good in the everyday awards, or those whom the administrators considered worthy of award.

The Icon Helpers system was launched for Newgrounds on June 27, 2006, for the volunteers to create and submit icons for the newer flash content for those which were lacking an icon, making the incorporation to automated collections pages which were much more effectual.

Tom was not just the creator of the website but was also the one to contribute regularly to the site by submitting several major flashes to the website. But most of the games that he created were violent and brutal in nature. For example Club-A-Seal, along with that he has also produced several games where children commit suicide, schools get attacked and many other such games which involved violence.

Since 2001, Fulp partnered with several other flash artists like Krinkels, Mockery, and Paladin to create different flash games. Fulp usually would program the games, while the other partners would make the art. Nevertheless, the quantity of games and movies that he submits on the site varies significantly from year to year, in 2004 he created only one game, whereas in 2006 he created eleven entries. In addition to that Tom also submitted two audio tracks and two pieces of art, which were not well received by the users.

Tom Fulp also co-created another video game company named The Behemoth, in 2002, in association with John Baez and Dan Paladin. The company's development studio is located at San Diego, California. The company produces video games with 2D style.

Along with being a programmer Fulp is also interested in music. During his freshman year, at the Drexel University, in Philadelphia, Fulp got interested in rave parties and decided to become a DJ, though for a short period of time.

On May 12, 2007, Tom got married to April Fulp, their first son Liam was born on March 25, 2009 and in July 2011, they became the parents of their second child. Tom's elder brother, Wade Fulp is in charge of the administration and handles several other issues that take place in Newgrounds.

DEEP KALRA,
FOUNDER & CHIEF EXECUTIVE OFFICER
OF MAKEMYTRIP.COM

Deep Kalra was working as a bank person in 1995 when he joined an American Company, AMF Bowling, to start billiards halls in India for first time. He quit his job and started expanding the company business to small centers and opened around 2000 play stations for bowling and billiards. Though it was not his own business, but he worked mostly on his own in establishing the business for a boss who was operating from US.

He was not yet satisfied and wanted to do something new on his own, so he again quit his job from AMF Bowling after working for 4 years. Kalra is one who dared to think different and achieved something which many people just dream of. He has sensed the might of internet technology and MakeMyTrip.com was the result of his experience he had earned through traveling. He was willing to simplify traveling and make a business out of it. He introduced a futuristic service MakeMyTrip.com.

The venture was something new for the people to accept at that time and they were not confident enough to put their money on this. Make people use their credit cards on an unknown entity was not going to be an easy thing to do. Reliability issues were in the minds of the people. Dot-com bubble also hindered the progress of the Internet business, and generating capital had become difficult for an internet venture. With all the problems, Kalra along with 2 managers decided to put their equity in the company and worked without salary for a long time. According to Kalra, "It worked out, so we can say we were resilient. But at that time I worried I was just being stubborn, but I figured you regret the things you don't do in life, not the things you do." [21]

The company now has gross revenue of US$ 5 million every year and total dealing value of US$ 500 million through bookings. Popularity of MakeMyTrip.com is now on its highest than ever, with one of twelve flights booked through MakeMyTrip.com. Though company generates most of the revenue through flight bookings, but train tickets also contribute a big chunk in it. According to the officials of the company, they sell 2500 train tickets every day. Now the company is planning to launch a public IPO of MakeMyTrip.com, but CEO, Deep Kalra, is not yet ready to reveal his cards.

On the other hand, Kalra is also ecstatic about the success of the company which was introduced at a time when he felt he was an alien in the world. According to him, it was a risk worth taking, because he was also tempted to jump into dot-com bandwagon. He also thought it took a much longer time to reach where it is now, but he is glad that he stayed here in India rather than going anywhere else, "If I'd been in Silicon Valley I'm convinced we might have reached scale in half the time, but we also probably would have been obliterated by the competition."[22]

Deep is rather qualified to manage an online travel company as he had studied in IIM Ahmedabad for his MBA (PGDBM) qualification. He is also an economics graduate from St. Stephen's College, Delhi.

MakeMyTrip.com also deals in hotel bookings, national and international, car rentals, visa services, B2B services, tourism packages for national and international tours. Right now, the company has established 20 offices across India as well as international offices in New York and San Francisco. Other than that, company also has several franchises. When Kalra started to think about it, he had in mind that this is the area which has been yet untouched and he knew how internet can play a big role in accessing these services from anywhere in India. He also knew that as the computing

---

[21] http://www.workhomemoney.com/entrepreneure-stories/makemytripcom-the-story-of-online-travel-booking-startup/

[22] http://blogalize.typepad.com/micro/2009/11/india-entrepreneur-makemytrip.html

technology is spreading, the market is getting bigger, and as the country is developing, more people will be able to use these services, it was just a matter of stabilizing and to take the right step at the right time for him.

He never lost confidence in his project even when all was looking doomed after dot-com bubble. He already had enough experience in the industry as how to survive during the toughest of the time which he learned when he was in GE Capital, working as Vice President of Business Development. Resources of Internet had not been extracted till then in India and he understood the process of Internet while he was with GE.

Travel sector in itself was a big business in India and he just mingled it with online services and this idea really excited him. The concept of MakeMyTrip.com came through then. Initially, the travel between America to India was their primary focus, as it had a huge potential to grow and it did happen as in a very short period of time, MakeMyTrip.com was one of the fastest growing venture in this sector. MakeMyTrip.com now holds on to 4% NRI market out of a total value of US$ 1 billion.

Development of Indian travel market specifically affected the business for good. Many low fare airlines were established, it encouraged Kalra to start an Indian MakeMyTrip.com and in 2005, they started operating in India. It became India's largest e-commerce company within one year. According to a survey in 2010, MakeMyTrip.com was India's number one travel company.

MakeMyTrip.com is a one-stop travel shop which offers various products and services such as international and domestic; air tickets, holiday packages, and hotel bookings, domestically; bus and train tickets, private car and taxi rentals, meetings, incentives, conferences, and exhibition services, as well as B2B and affiliate services. These offers are being executed through the website of the company MakeMyTrip.com. Other than that, there are 20 branches which are performing well for the business along with the new franchise outlets across India. The company is also managing 24x7 call centers to help the customers.

Company's Board of directors is a blend of independent member as well as investors. SAIF Partners, Helion Venture Partners, and Sierra Ventures are the financial investors for the company. Some well-established entrepreneurs and professionals complete the list of independent board members such as Frederic Lalonde, founder and CEO of Openplaces. org, Sanjeev Bikhchandani, CEO and Founder of Info Edge (India) Ltd., Philip C. Wolf, President and CEO of PhoCusWright Inc.

MakeMyTrip.com has received a number of awards for its contribution in travel and business sector as well as airlines sector. A long list of awards comprises Red Herring 100 Asia in 2007, Superbrand India in 2009, Great Places To Work in 2009, Most Preferred/Best Travel Portal by CNBC Awaaz in 2009, Most Visited Travel Website by comScore from 2005-09, Most Preferred Online Travel Agency by Travel Biz Monitor Survey in 2008, Number One Online Travel Agency from JuxtConsult in 2008, Gold and Silver by Abby Award in 2006-07, Among the Top Ten Websites visited by Indians by comScore in 2007, Nominated World Travel Awards by Asia's Leading Travel Agency in 2007, Among 100 IT Innovators judged by NASSCOM in 2007, Best Online Travel Company by Galileo Express Travel World in 2007, Emerging India Award by ICICI Bank & CNBC TV18 in 2006, Asia's Hottest Technology Startup by Red Herring in 2006. All these awards were given for company's work in travel and business sectors.

While the company also got quite a few awards for their work in travel sector which includes an award given by Air Canada for Outstanding Performance in 2008, Singapore Airlines awarded for Top Passenger Agent in 2007-08, an award by British Airways for Outstanding Revenue Contribution in 2007-08, All India Top Ten Agent//Top North India Sales Award by Air Mauritius through 2006-07/2007-08, Outstanding Performance award by Cathay Pacific in 2007, Top Agent Award by Malaysia Airlines in 2007, Outstanding Performance Lufthansa by Lufthansa in 2006-07, also awarded by Kingfisher Airlines for an Outstanding Performance in 2006-07, an award by Indian Airlines for Achieving Highest Domestic Passenger Sales in 2006-07, Outstanding Contribution to Passenger Sales award by Air India in 2005-06, Award of Excellence by Jet Airways in 2005-06, and one more award by Gulf Air for Continuous Support.

The company has adopted a Hybrid OTA Model in regards to their business expansion. They have established 20 regional offices across the country and also worked on franchise system to take it far and to smaller cities. Travel experts sitting in those franchisees discuss with the people interested in traveling face to face and make it easy for them to decide the best package which is perfectly fit for them. This helps customers who like direct interaction in comparison to talk on phone, online chat, or e-mails.

MakeMyTrip.com partnered with Amadeus IT Group for technological developments in February 2007 and also started a joint process with Nokia for the customers to book air tickets via mobile phones. Though company claims for the best services for the customers, but still criticisms happened as the company was accused for not giving its customers complete independent choices about luggage, option of changing travel date, or cancel the ticket before ticket bookings. Company is also blamed for showing low priority for attending calls for booked tickets in comparison to calls to purchase tickets. Seeking help from company's call center for a booked ticket is a headache for customers. Credit card refunding is another process which gets delayed sometimes.

Andrew Gower,
Founder of RuneScape,
The world's most popular free
online multiplayer game

Andrew Gower was born in Nottingham, England, on 2 December 1978. Gower is a video game developer who co-founded Jagex Games Studio based in Cambridge. This company was founded along with Paul Gower and Constant Tedder. He is a UK-based entrepreneur. He and his brother Paul Gower together wrote MMORPG RuneScape. He quit the position of board of directors, Jagex, in December 2010. He is still working there as a principal architect.

Andrew Gower went to The Becket School and after that he joined Cambridge University for further studies. According to Sunday Times, in 2007, Gower brothers had assets were worth £113 million and were 654th richest entrepreneurs in the UK. Though in 2009, they went down on that list of Sunday Times at 566th with an estimated £99 million. They were ranked at number 11 in a list of richest young entrepreneurs by Daily Telegraph in the UK.

Andrew Gower with the help of his brother Paul Gower released RuneScape in January 2001 which is a massively multiplayer online role-playing game (MMORPG). The game is developed under the name of Jagex Games Studio. RuneScape has been developed in Java and implemented on the client-side. This is a graphical browser game which also runs on 3D. This online game gets an estimated 10 million user accounts every month and boats of a total registered account of 156 millions. RuneScape is awarded by the Guinness World Records as the most popular MMORPG in the world.

RuneScape is created around Gielinor, which is a medieval world of fantasy, consisted of different kingdoms, regions, and cities. Players can use magical teleportation spells and devices to walk through Gielinor on foot. Other method for travel is charter ships. We also find different resources, monsters, and their challenges as we go along on different regions. There is another website for the game to get more information about this fictional universe that is, FunOrb, Armies of Gielinor. Reading the novels Betrayal at Falador and Return to Canifis will make you more assure about your prospects when playing the game.

RuneScape was initially though, like a MUD based on text, but it was developed with graphics from the start and then was known as a "graphical MUD." The 3-D and 2-D programming was used to develop the first launched version of the game and then the beta version was released on January 4, 2001. Gower brother used their parents' house to develop and operate the game as a startup which was in Nottingham.

In December 2001, Jagex was established to look into the business aspect of the game by Gower brothers in company with Constant Tedder. Jagex worked on language development for games. The first one was an "interpreted domain-specific scripting language" named RuneScript. This script was used to develop RuneScape server. A monthly membership was planned and introduced on February 27, 2002. In this service, there were some new features which were not available for free users as well as accessing to new areas and quest was enabled.

With more users on their databases, Jagex started making some changes to the game. Game was rewritten again with a complete 3D approach and was launched which was given a name RuneScape 2. A special beta version of RuneScape 2 was also released on December 1, 2003, for paid users the period of which ended on March 29, 2004. The game was set for testing during this period. When the new version of the game was released, the old version was renamed as RuneScape Classic and was available online while the new version was again given the same name the RuneScape.

In a dramatic event, Jagex was banned for around 5000 RuneScape Classic users for using the game because of some wrong doings. Later, Classic version of the game was only available for some selected users who had played it in between August 3, 2005 to January 12, 2006 and it was closed for new accounts.

Free version of RuneScape was aided by the advertisements which are shown on a banner above the playing screen for the users. Free users can only play RuneScape when their browsers do not automatically block the advertisements shown on the site through pop-up blockers. This rule was announced to encourage the advertisers. A business deal between Jagex and WildTangent Games also came to fore on July 13, 2006. By virtue of the deal, WildTangent Games got the rights for advertising management of RuneScape in USA. WildTangent Games Network will also distribute the RuneScape game to reach more than over 20 million users.

The game engine of RuneScape was updated on May 16, 2006. Purpose of this update was to decrease the requirement of memory by increasing its loading time. One more feature of Future Content was added in another update on June 26, 2007. Beta version of "High Detail" mode was released on July 1, 2008, initially only for paid service but was then opened for free users as well after two 2 weeks. This version was revealed at E3 trade show before its launch in 2008.

Company in September 2009 decided to reopen RuneScape Classic for free users with one additional feature where the users could take their own server to administer on rent. It allowed them to banning of unwanted users and could also enable and disable the cheat codes. This announcement was canceled only after two months and it was not even implemented at that time. But on November 11, 2009, they again opened it for the duration of two weeks for the members. It was then closed after two weeks and again opened on June 1, 2010, for the users who had logged into it in that two-week time period in 2009. A cape was added for every user who had logged into the classic version of the game even once on May 3, 2011.

There was an interview of Geoff Iddison, former Jagex CEO, in May 2008, former who said that, "We do plan to go East with RuneScape to the Asian market and the Eastern European market too." He further stated that, "RuneScape is not for Japan, but it could work well in Malaysia for example and where is India in all this? I think RuneScape is a game that would be adopted in the English-speaking Indian world and the local-speaking Indian world. We're looking at all those markets individually."

Zapak gaming portal launched RuneScape in India on October 8, 2009. It came out in France and Germany on 27 May 2010 and was launched by through Bigpoint Games.

As April 2011 passed, RuneScape had established game servers all over the world. A total number of 172 RuneScape servers have already been setup by now. These Jagex user and players call these servers as worlds. The locations for these servers are United Kingdom, United States, Canada, Netherlands, Australia, Sweden, Finland, Belgium, Ireland, Norway, Denmark, New Zealand, Mexico, France, Lithuania, and India. These servers help users to experience an ultimate gaming experience with fast and uninhibited connection. Also, availability of a large number of servers makes them very cost effective tool.

At once, about 2000 users can log into a single RuneScape server and can use the server to the fullest. Total capacity of RuneScape servers goes up to 340,000 logs simultaneously. Servers are also categorized as free and paid servers. Free servers are available for every user and paid member services are managed through different paid servers.

Three of those servers are dedicated to RuneScape Classic. RuneScape also developed to give language options to the players. English is the primary language for the game servers though there are servers which translate the game into different languages like two servers for French, five servers for German, and six servers for Brazilian Portuguese.

RuneScape has an excellent graphic supports with various types of graphic software. Graphical details are important when we differentiate different graphic platforms which help enhancing the gaming experience for players. High detail graphics makes the game look better in texture and design while low detail graphics gives a neater look to the game and reduce the response on slow computers. "RuneTek 5" is a graphic engine used for RuneScape.

It enables users to use multiple graphics applications like video game consoles, DirectX, and OpenGL. Various graphical effects can also be used without much fuss. It supports sky boxes, bloom lighting, and Z-buffering. The high-detail graphical software helps in hardware acceleration and Java OpenGL or DirectX can be used to operate it.

A character-customization system is an important element in a RuneScape game. This feature differentiates RuneScape to other MMORPG based games as only human characters can be customized here, though players get the different options for these human characters like gender, hairstyles, body type, facial features, skin color, and different clothing options. Wearing and wielding options certainly complement the character's appearances. Specially developed emotes can be used to show emotions by the players through there customized characters. Some standard ammunitions and weapons like swords along with some unique kind of special weapons in a whole make the game exciting and interesting for the players.

RuneScape also contains real sound effects which make it an amazing gaming experience and addition of music and synthesizer makes it even better. Players can hear ambient noises when in Gielinor. Music score complements the situation and location very beautifully. It let the players know about every moment that is happening in the game.

On the RuneScape website, users can also find official forums developed by Jagex. These forums give players a chance to participate in discussions about the game. Users can also take part in forum games which are made by player. Different items can also be bought and sold through these forums. Users can also post their suggestions about the game as what it is lacking in. Poll options enable users tell about their choice about a specific question asked by the company on this website. Users communicate with each other and can be indulged in several other activities as well. RuneScape though contains less feature sets in comparison to other MMORPG forums.

User Avatar can be created with a separate display name, though automatic signatures cannot be set on this forum. Users can see the number of posts they have done in the user profiles as well as an option of disabling smileys is also available. A few user friendly options of text formatting, image display, and links posting is now allowed. Posting access is only limited to premium members of RuneScape along with those members who have crossed 350 levels in the game.

Players though got a chance to ask questions through e-mail between September 24, 2002 to December 9, 2004, which were answered by the RuneScape Gods. These e-mails were published as letters on the forum. One more feature "Postbag from the Hedge" was added on September 26, 2005. This feature gave users a right to send e-mail to a non-player character in the game. They also made it possible for players to post their RuneScape artwork based on related artwork which are displayed on RuneScape website in a gallery.

Jagex organizes special events in a specific location that is on Gielinor on holidays like Easter, April Fools, Thanksgiving, Halloween, and Christmas. If during the event a player completes the task given, they reward the player with emote or an item. These emotes are used to express emotions and gestures by the characters. Before 2002, the items awarded during holidays were worth a significant amount of money and could be out on trading to earn money on the player market. Holidays items awarded to players after Christmas 2002 cannot be put on sale and player can only get one item and if a player lost an item, it can also be retrieved.

RuneScape players have established several fansites for RuneScape where people can know more about the game. Initially, the official website of RuneScape had links in it to several fansites, but the official website removed those links after some time. Knowledge Base was introduced by Jagex in order to give them additional information about gaming. RuneScape rules when it comes to the security of account. Players cannot discuss about the game on fansites or the official forums while playing the game at the same time. This practice has been discouraged for security reasons. According to this, sharing web addresses is prohibited. Jagex has also been criticized because of these rules by a major fansite of RuneScape for not giving credit to the fansites for their contribution is popularizing and development of the game.

Though, in 2009, Jagex stated that they will try to increase communication with the fansites. Players are also informed about the rules and regulation about players' conduct and behavior. Players cannot use abusive language, scamming, and bug abuse. There is also a function available for the players to report about any abuse or if any rule is broken by any player. It helps RuneScape to enforce the rules in a much better fashion.

RuneScape uses moderators to follow the activities of the players and keep them in check. Three kind of moderator are there to keep a check on the activities of the players one is the Jagex moderator, who is an appointed employee of Jagex, another one is player moderators, these are players of RuneScape who are trusted to enforce the rules, and also Forum Moderators, in this section forums are watched carefully by trusted players. Players can also be permanently or temporarily banned from playing games if they continuously break the rules of conduct. However, if banned players pay a specific amount, they can be disbanded again.

Some of the rules prohibit using third-party software while playing the game. These types of software are known as macroing. Players also cannot trade or sell game items to earn money in the market. Jagex also put a lot of effort to stop cheating in the game. They also made rules to stop false practices.

Jagex released update to stop real world trades in between October 2007 to December 2007. This update restricted users to trade more than specified items. Player-versus-play combat was also removed, which gave a power of invisibility to a valuable player Gravestones were added for the dead players items, started a grand exchange pretty much like in a share market kind of method, created a system to distribute loots, and to enhance the players skills and knowledge about the game. Though player-versus-player combat and unbalanced trading features were restarted again on February 1, 2011, after a poll asking to vote for these and it got 1.2 million in its favor, total 91% RuneScape voters preferred these options.

There are essential and attractive game elements in RuneScape such as skills, combat, player interaction, and non-player interaction.

There are 25 different kinds of skills to perform activities in the game. Many of these skills are mining, cooking, wood cutting, fishing, fletching, selling, stealing, hunting, and planting of plants, etc. Players' skill level determines the total score and status of the players in the game. With more skills, players can perform tasks better and can get more raw materials.

Skill experience is also an important aspect as it increases the level of characters. When a player achieves the highest skill level, player will be awarded by special cape called as "Cape of Accomplishment" or a "Skill Cape." These awards are given to recognize the players' achievement. Moreover, a "Max Cape" can also be purchased if players reach at highest skill levels in all skills.

RuneScape combat is a real time combat system developed by the developers. In this section, players fight with other creatures and players to get items or gold. Combat level of the player shows the power of a player in the game.

Player versus player combat is performed in an area called as Wilderness. Players can also put money and items on stake in Duel Arena. Players combat each other if their combat levels are in a certain range from one another.

Some non-player characters also come into play in the game. These NPCs are like monsters. These monsters are categorized form small to big such as from chicken and goblin to Kalphite Queen, Corporeal Beast, TzTok-Jad, or King Black Dragon which are big monsters. These monsters can attack the players and they also posses their strengths and weaknesses. There are also two types of monsters such as aggressive and non-aggressive. Aggressive monsters can attack on regular basis at any time, while non-aggressive monsters only attack if they are prompted. These monsters make some dangerous areas while walking on Gielinor.

Chatting, trading, mini-games, and other activities are used for interaction between the players. These methods can also be competitive or combative while some will need cooperation and collective effort to perform. Trading can also be done through trade items and gold coins on a face-to-face interaction or through the share market called "Grand Exchange."

There are some story-specific tasks too which players can choose to perform, these are known as Quests. Quests require players to have certain skills level and combat levels along with some quests can only be performed if players have completed some other specific quests or they have quest points. After completing questions players are rewarded by prizes such as unique items, access to new areas, money, skills experience, and money. An award names "Quest Point Cape" is also given to a player who completes all the quests of the game.

There were few controversies against the free player-versus-player combat. On 10 December, 2007, there were a few updates by Jagex that real currencies were being traded in these games instead of the virtual goods that were being used in the games. Many of the members actively complained about the whole thing and the site lost several of its users. But it did not affect the site as much as the owners were expecting it to be.

RYAN BLOCK
FOUNDER OF WWW.ENGADGET.COM

Ryan Block works as a technology journalist and critic. He worked with AOL as an editor-in-chief for their program called Engadget. He co-founded a technology community site named gdgt.

Ryan Block is from Southern California originally and in 2001, he moved from California to Jersey City, New Jersey, but his stay there could stretch for only two to three months as he was also trying to find a place to live in New York. He spent quite a few years of his in Manhattan and Brooklyn as well.

He started working as a part-timer for a technology news website Engadget in June 2004 and became a full-time reporter in June 2005. Thereafter, in 2007 he became the editor-in-chief of Engadget replacing Peter Rojas who created the site. In an incident, Block wrote about a leaked e-mail about the delay of iPhone and Mac OS X Leopard on May 16, 2007, and according to some reports this affected Apple market for about $4 billion in a very short period of time, even though Apple declared the e-mail is fake. Block later revealed that he has followed the market after he explained that the e-mail was actually fake and also found that the $4 billion drop in the market was restored immediately.

Block announced to quit the position of editor-in-chief for Engadget in July 2008, as he was going to start his own company. After him Joshua Topolsky, the Associate Editor of Engadget took over the position. He along with Rojas collected some first series finance of $550,000 from Betaworks and True Ventures to start their new company and launched gdgt. Gdgt is a discussion forum which generates users and expert about different gadgets. Users also seek for answers of their questions on the site.

Block has appeared on The Engadget Show to state his views as a panelist. As well as, he made his appearance on the show "This Week in Tech" of Leo Laporte for about 21 times.

Ryan Block now lives with his girlfriend Veronica Belmont in San Francisco, California. Engadget, where Block worked as an Editor-in-chief is a multilingual technology website. This site covers gadgets and consumer electronic products. Engadget is pretty much like an online magazine which works in a blog fashion. Engadget have created 10 blogs to work on right now. Four of those ten blogs are published in English language while other six are international blogs written by independent experts. Techanori top 100 has ranked Engadget at number 5. In 2010, TIME has declared Engadget one of the best blogs of the year.

Though Block worked as an editor-in-chief at Engadget but Peter Rojas was the man who co-founded the site. Prior to this, Rojas worked as a technology editor at Gizmodo. Engadget was actually established as a member of Weblogs, Inc. More than 75 web blogs are working under this company such as Autoblog and Joystiq. In 2005, AOL acquired the Weblogs Inc.

Ryan Block on July 22, 2008, announced to quit from his post of editor-in-chief for Engadget in by late August. Joshua Topolsky became the new editor-in-chief. Joshua Topolsky too announced about quitting Engadget on March 12, 2011, and his chair will be taken by Tim Stevens as he leaves.

Engadget blogs are written in seven languages like English, German, Korean, Chinese, Spanish, Polish, and Japanese. Four blogs are dedicated for English version of Engadget and these blogs are assimilated in a single site home page. These Engadget blogs have been given names like Engadget Classic, Engadget Mobile, Engadget HD, and Engadget Alt.

Company updates Engadget blogs several times every day and post articles related to gadgets and consumer electronics. Engadget was launched in 2004. Engadget also informs readers about the rumors and possibilities in tech world. They ask for polls and opinions of readers about the tech gadgets. Users can also listen to their Engadget Podcast every week.

Several tech expert and writers have posted articles and comments on the blogs since it has been founded. There are different blogs provided for different tech inventions like Engadget classic, Engadget Alt, Engadget Mobile, and Engadget HD. Several professional journalists, industry tech analysts, and renowned bloggers have contributed to make Engadget engaging. A few writers who worked on Engadget are Joshua Fruhlinger, Jason Calacanis, Susan Mernit, Paul Boutin, Darren Murph, Phillip Torrone, Marc Perton, and Nilay Patel. Amongst them, Darren Murph was tagged by Guinness World Records on July 29, 2010, as the World's Most Prolific Professional Blogger. He right now is working as an associate editor for Engadget. He writes an enormous amount of posts and has already written about 17,212 articles till date. Ross Rubin, an Industry analyst, writes one column per week for Engadget named Switched On and is writing his articles since October 2004.

Because of their fantastic work in tech arena, Engadget have been appreciated by award functions as it was nominated for Bloggie for Best Technology Weblog in 2004 and in 2005 Bloggies for Best Computers or Technology Weblog and Best Group Weblog. Engadget has already won Best Tech Blog award in the 2004 and Weblog Awards of 2005.

Engadget has been included by Google Reader and many other RSS readers as their default RSS feed to read their articles on gadgets and tech world. The content of Engadget is published in Blogsmith CMS font.

In October 2004, Engadget launched podcast which Phillip Torrone and Len Pryor hosted together initially for the first 22 episodes of the podcast. Later, Eric Rice started hosting the podcast who also had his own podcast named The Eric Rice Show, though he could only host Engadget podcast for 4 episodes, when Ryan Block and Peter Rojas themselves starting hosting it. Joshua Topolsky, who became Editor-in-chief later, and other editors of Engadget like Paul Miller and Nilay Patel together too hosted some of the occasional podcast with special guests before they all departed in 2011. Trent Wolbe was producing the podcast which was edited by Topolsky and right now Tim Stevens, the new editor-in-chief of Engadget is looking after it.

Engadget podcast is created to talk about technology, new gadgets, rumors, new products, and company status related to technology or about any new announcement by the companies. The show comes out once a week and goes for duration of mostly an hour. Now and then we can also find more than one podcast a week on some special occasions or events like Electronic Entertainment Expo or Consumer Electronics Show (CES). Sometimes during these events, podcast comes out on a daily basis.

To subscribe for an Engadget podcast, people need to sign for marketplace, iTunes, or Zune Marketplace. It is also available as an RSS feed. Net users can also download it directly from Engadget website in different audio formats like, Ogg, mp3, m4b, or AAC. User can also see the pictures of the topic or product discussed by downloading m4b format and also can be seen via iTunes or on a player which supports this format. Now days, live podcasts are also broadcasted on Ustream Engadget. It has started doing live on Thursday or Friday afternoons. The recorded podcast will be available to download next day of the live podcast.

Engadget also released their first mobile application on December 30, 2009, for the iPhone and iPod touch. This application has features like Twitter and Facebook integration to share their articles. Articles could also be sent through e-mail. Bookmark and view offline features were also added in the application. With breaking news option, they ensured that the users do not miss any news from Engadget.

Engadget application for Palm Pre and Palm Pixie phones was released on January 1, 2010, as "1000th application for PalmOS users." After a week, the app was launched on the BlackBerry platform on January 8, 2010. On March 25, 2010, an Android was also released by the company to complete a set of mobile applications available on most smart phones OS.

On September 8, 2009, a production of new video show was announced by CEO, Josh Topolsky, which will be shot in New York City with free audience entries and video of the show will be available on the Engadget website too. Attraction of the show was one-on-one interview with experts. It also had a short videos segment with live music included and a roundtable discussions round about technology. The first episode was filmed in Parsons "The New School for Design" at Tishman Auditorium where it was shot for first four episodes and then was shifted to in New York Times Building at their Times Center.

Joshua Topolsky, then editor-in-chief, along with sub-editors, Paul Miller and Nilay Patel, together hosted this show originally. Later, Tom Stevens, new EIC, took the responsibility to host the show as Topolsky left Engadget and AOL in 2011. The director of the show is Michelle Stahl. Joshua Fruhlinger and Michael Rubens are associated with the show as executive producers.

Engadget has also been involved in some controversies as well, as in 2006, it was reported that Engadget's name was used by a mall in Kuala Lumpur, Malaysia, which they denied to take any action for as a good gesture from the Engadget owners. The name of that store has been changed though and is opened with a new name somewhere else. In another similar kind of incident, there was another store, which was seen on July 2007 using a logo pretty similar to the logo of Engadget.

Engadget landed on to another controversy in May 2007 when a fake e-mail which was reporting about an Apple employee stated that both the iPhone and Mac OS X Leopard will delayed to launch. This story affected Apple's market a lot and its shares were down up to 3%. Later it was found that the e-mail was fraud and was removed from the Engadget website and, them CEO, Ryan had to apologize about this hoax which enabled Apples Shares to recover.

In another controversy, in 2006, a digital audio players website, DAPreview found a picture used in Engadget that was taken by DAPreview. DAPreview also claimed that the credentials of the like logo of DAPreview was cropped and edited before posting the picture. DAPreview raised this issue, but Ryan Block solely accepted their mistake and apologized. That image was then posted in its original form again with DAPreview logo on it.

On March 31, 2008, a report came out from Engadget according to which Deutsche Telekom, owners of T-Mobile and T-Mobile USA, had requested the editors of Engadget to remove magenta color from their Mobile site. T-Mobile explained that they had the copyright trademark of this color. Engadget responded and repainted their site and also changed the mobile logo for a day which quite resembled like "Engadge t-mobile". It stayed like this for a day only before they went back into the old format and color scheme excluding the highlighting color. Engadget was awarded for their "The Engadget Show" 2011 with People's Voice Webby Award in Consumer Electronics.

The year 2011 though proved an incidental time for Engadget as it saw a mass exit as several editorial team members, as well as technical staff left Engadget and moved to SB Nation to work with Jim Bankoff and started a new gadget website. Joshua Topolsky explained the side of quitting members saying that, "We have been working on blogging technology that was developed in 2003, we haven't made a hire since I started running the site, and I thought we could be more successful elsewhere".

Several important members of Engadget including Topolsky, Ross Miller, Joanna Stern, Nilay Patel, Chris Ziegler, and Paul Miller, left the company. The reason behind this was supposed to be "an internal memo" that was given by AOL to their employees which was called "The AOL Way." This memo contained 58-pages describing they are trying to change AOL into a media empire. Employees accused AOL to destroy journalism for their ambitious business plans.

Their plans to increase page views and advertisements to increase revenues will affect the impartial reporting of Engadget. Paul Miller also talked about this and wrote in his blog, "I'd love to be able to keep doing this forever, but unfortunately Engadget is owned by AOL, and AOL has proved an unwilling partner in this site's evolution. It doesn't take a veteran of the publishing world to realize that AOL has its heart in the wrong place with content. As detailed in the "AOL Way," and borne out in personal experience, AOL sees content as a commodity it can sell ads against."

STEVE JOBS FOUNDER OF APPLE CORP

Steven Paul Jobs aka "Steve" Jobs was born in San Francisco, California on February 24, 1955. Steve Jobs is a business magnate in America who also likes to invent new things and offer to the people by launching in the market. He co-founded Apple Inc. and also serves as a chief executive officer there. Steve Jobs has also been the CEO of Pixar Animation Studios previously and in 2006, he also joined the board of directors of The Walt Disney Company as Disney acquired Pixar Animation. A film named Toy Story that came in 1995, Steve Jobs worked as an executive producer on that.

Steve Jobs partnered with his Apple co-founder Steve Wozniak and Mike Markkula and developed as well as designed the first series of personal computers in late 1970s. These PCs became a huge success commercially and got popular. These personal computers were called Apple II series, but these computers were not graphically supportive and were used without mouse, though Jobs sensed the potential success and started developing more advanced graphical computers in early 1980s. He then developed Macintosh. Although in 1984, Jobs had to resign from Apple after a power dispute with the board of directors.

After that Jobs started a computer platform development company, NeXT which was specialized in higher education and business markets. Steve Jobs came back to Apple in 1996. A computer graphics division called Lucasfilm Ltd was also acquired by him in 1986 which was then renamed Pixar Animation Studios. He had the majority shares of the Pixar at 50.1% and stayed as the CEO until it was acquired in 2006 by The Walt Disney Company. As a result of the acquisition, Jobs was left with most of the individual shares in Disney and joined their Board of Directors.

Jobs' presence at the Silicone Valley created an identity with his name, and his business concepts and idiosyncratic approach established him a successful entrepreneur. He worked on individual needs and gave immense importance to design products which attract people collectively and are efficient in working capacity. His motive has been to develop elegant as well as highly user friendly products.

Paul and Clara Jobs adopted him when he was born and gave him a name Steven Paul. They also adopted a girl whom they named Patti. Abdulfattah Jandali and Joanne Simpson are the biological parents of Steve jobs. Abdulfattah Jandali is a Syrian-origin who was a graduate student and went on to work as a political science professor, while Joanne Simpson is an American who also was a graduate student and then became a speech language pathologist. They both married and gave a birth to another child, a girl, biological sister of Jobs Moan Simpson; she is a well known novelist now.

Jobs studied at Cupertino Junior High School and Homestead High School in Cupertino, California. He used to go to Hewlett-Packard Company in Palo Alto, California, to learn about technology after school. He was then employed by the company as a summer employee and worked with Steve Wozniak. He graduated from high school in 1972 and entered Reed College in Portland, Oregon, but after only semester, he left the university.

He started attending auditing classes at Reed College and was staying with his friends. He slept on the floor there and collected empty coke bottles to return to earn money. He used to go to Hare Krishna temple to get free meals. Jobs himself says, "If I had never dropped in on that single course in college, the Mac would have never had multiple typefaces or proportionally spaced fonts".

In 1974, Jobs and Wozniak started participating in the meetings of Homebrew Computer Club as he returned back California. He also worked at Atari as a technician. Atari is a popular video developer. His intent was to earn money to go to India for spiritual and mediation purposes.

After saving enough money, he traveled to India. He also accompanied a friend from reed College his who also became first employee for Apple and Daniel Kottke. Their purpose was to look into spirituality and awaken their inner soul. When he came back from India, he was changed he had shaved his head like a Buddhist and was using traditional Indian clothes. Jobs also tested psychedelics and called it LSD experience and said that, "one of the two or three most important things he had done in his life" He described that he found that his thinking had changed and many people were not able to connect to his thinking.

Jobs after coming back to USA rejoined Atari. There, he was handed over a job of creating circuit board for a new game called Breakout. This task turned to be an interesting story. Jobs was offered $100 for each chip he remove from the board. Though Jobs had no knowledge about chips or designing a circuit board, but he talked to Wozniak and offered him divide the amount even between the two. Wozniak then worked on the board and eliminated 50 chips from the board. It was an amazing work done by Wozniak and he reduced the number of chips so much that it had become a small and congested and was hard to re-manufacture on the production line. As a result, Atari only paid $700 to jobs for this work which Jobs shard with Wozniak in half.

Steve jobs and Wozniak then came together with Ronald Wayne and AC Markkula, an Intel product-marketing manager and engineer who funded them for the venture introduced Wozniak was an electronics hacker before co-founding Apple. Jobs and Wozniak met each other in 1971 and had been friends since then. At the time of meeting, Wozniak was 21 year old while Jobs was only 16 and they were introduced by a mutual friend Bill Fernandez.

Mike Scott was hired by Apple to work as a CEO, in 1978, who also worked as National Semiconductor, but his appointment proved to be chaotic for Apple and at last in 1983, Steve Jobs was able to excite John Sculley to join Apple as a CEO who was working with Pepsi-Cola at that time. Steve Jobs just asked a simple question, "Do you want to sell sugar water for the rest of your life, or do you want to come with me and change the world?" A Super Bowl television commercial came out from Apple in 1984, the title was also "1984."

Jobs introduced Macintosh on January 24, 1984, in an annual shareholders meeting with an emotional speech in front of a large and exciting audience. Scenes at this event were called as "pandemonium" by Andy Hertzfeld. The Macintosh computer was created with graphical user interface and mouse click operation. It was one of its kind successful small size computers at that time containing graphical user interface. Jef Raskin was the man who started developing Mac which later accomplished by Steve jobs.

Though Job had yielded great results for Apple as a director with efficient management skills, but he was known as a temperamental person among his employees of Apple. In 1984, during a market slump as sales of the company took a huge pounding, a dispute had developed between Jobs and Sculley, the CEO, and late next year it converted into a power struggle between the two and then in May 1985, company also relieved many a employees along with Jobs as the position of head of the Macintosh division was taken away from him.

After quitting from Apple, jobs created a new company named NeXT Computer where he designed another powerful work station similar to Apple Lisa, but more powerful though more expensive as well and because of its high cost, industry had dismissed it initially, but the people who could afford it, appreciated it because of the technological efficiency and a new additional development called object-oriented software development system. Jobs' marketing strategy was clear regarding the products of NeXT and that was to popularize them in scientific and academic institution.

At the NeXT, he was aimed to concentrate on innovation. There was an urge to experiment and invent new products. Some of the new advanced technology stuff came out from them were built-in Ethernet port, Mach kernel, and the digital signal processor chip.

Another development that came out from NeXT was a distinct computer called NeXTcube, which Jobs described as an "interpersonal" computer, next stage of development after "personal" computers, according to Jobs. Jobs' purpose behind this development was to replace personal computer to allow people to communication using a computing solution in an easy way.

Steve Jobs also bought a company called Pixar in 1986 for $10 million. Before it was known as a Graphic group and was working under from Lucasfilm's computer graphics division. Pixar was originally operating in San Rafael, California, at Lucasfilm's Kerner Studios, but after the acquisition, it was the shifted to Emeryville, California. This company started working as a high-end graphics hardware developer to start with and sold Pixar Image Computer, but was not able to earn much profit with those products. So, they decided to have a business deal with Disney, in which, they would make features films based on computer and Disney also showed interest to co-finance the films.

This collaboration came out with "Toy Story" in 1995 which was their first film produced together and the film proved to a commercial success and also getting critics appreciation. The partnership proved beneficiary for both the companies and they had realized a huge business potential of entertainment section.

Under the guidance of John Lasseter, creative chief of Pixar, company produced several successful films in the next ten years such as, "A Bug's Life in 1998, Toy Story 2 in 1999, Monsters, Inc. in 2001, Finding Nemo in 2003, The Incredibles in 2004, Cars in 2006, Ratatouille in 2007, WALL-E in 2008, Up in 2009, and Toy Story 3 in 2010. A few of these films like "Finding Nemo, The Incredibles, Ratatouille, WALL-E, Up, and Toy Story 3" were awarded with the "Academy Award for Best Animated Feature."

The contract that took place between Pixar and Disney was going to end in 2003-2004, and at that time Jobs and Michael Eisner, CEO Disney, talked about the renewal of the contract but was failed because of some issues. After contract had ended, in early 2004, Jobs started searching for a new partner to distribute their films.

Michael Eisner was replaced by Bob Iger in October 2005 as a CEO of Disney who started working towards making the relationship better with Steve Jobs and finally after settling the issues, an announcement was made on January 24, 2006, that Disney is purchasing Pixar completely for $7.4 billion. After this deal, Jobs had 7% shares of the Disney in his hand which enabled him to become the largest individual share holder.

Jobs then joined company's board of directors after collaboration of the two companies. Before Jobs, Michael Isner held the highest 1.7% shares of the company while Roy E. Disney had 1% shares. It was Roy Disney who criticized Micheal Isner for making the relationship between Pixar and Disney worse which became the reason for Isner's exit as CEO. Other than that, Jobs also is one of the six members of a committee which look after the animation business of Disney and Pixar.

In 1996, it came out that Apple is going acquire NeXT for estimated $429 million of payment. The deal came to reality soon at the end of 1996 which brought back Steve Jobs again to the company he had co-founded. Shortly after the acquisition, he was appointed as the interim CEO of the Apple which was the consequence of a boardroom coup between board members and Gil Amelio, CEO of Apple at that time. After some time, as he took over the CEO chair, Jobs decided to terminate a few projects named OpenDoc, Newton, and Cyberdog. The purpose behind this was to get the company back to profitability by developing some revenue gaining projects. It was then that many employees had developed a misconception about Jobs inconsistent and temperamental behavior.

The kind of fear he had created in employees was immense, as they did not even prepare to stand alongside him in an elevator, "afraid that they might not have a job when the doors opened. The reality was that Jobs' summary executions were rare, but a handful of victims were enough to terrorize a whole company." Macintosh clones' licensing program was also changed by Jobs which made it hard for manufacturers to produce machine because of cost constraints.

As NeXT was already acquired by Apple, the development happened in NeXT as an individual company were also absorbed by Apple, like in the case of NeXTSTEP. Apple developed NeXTSTEP further and renamed it as Mac OS X. Jobs worked on increasing the profit for the company and to be able to do that, company introduced new like iMac which helped them achieve the target of increasing sales and popularity. Jobs emphasized on creating eye-catching products designs and branding of Apple to popularize the company's name among the people which yielded great results. When Macworld Expo was organized in 2000, Jobs turned into a permanent CEO of Apple removing his "interim" tag.

Under the able guidance of Jobs, Apple has spread its business to various corners of the world, indulging themselves in consumer electronic products like a portable music player called iPod, also developed a digital music software iTunes, and opened iTunes Store to distribute the music. Jobs vision and experimental ideas took Apple into mobile phone development and Apple launched their first multi-touch smart phone called iPhone in 2007 which contained all the features of iPod and also consisting an all new web browser.

This mobile phone proved a revolutionary product for Apple n terms of web browsing experience of users. Though Jobs agenda has been new innovations and creative designs, but he also talks about "real artists ship" to his employees, means, product must be delivered at the right time with sharpest punctuality to keep the interest going without letting the people to much or think about the product.

Apple was also criticized by environmentalist for a poor recycling program and in an annual meeting of Apple, Jobs responded to all those critics and dismissed their allegations of not managing e-waste well enough. Later, after a few weeks, it was announced by Apple that old iPods can be returned back for free at Apple's retail stores for recycling. The Computer TakeBack Campaign was going in full flow and while commencing an event at Stanford University graduation, they flew a banner from a plane which had "Steve, Don't be a mini-player recycle all e-waste" written on it. Later Apple extended their area of recycling in 2006 and offered that US customers, who buy an Apple computer, can deliver the old one for recycling.

Jobs only take $1 a year as his salary, but he owns 5.426 million Apple shares as well as holds 138 million shares of Disney which takes his total gross worth up to $5.1 billion by 2009. He was ranked as 43rd in US in terms of total estimated asset. He said, "I was worth over $1,000,000 when I was 23, and over $10,000,000 when I was 24, and over $100,000,000 when I was 25, and it wasn't that important because I never did it for the money." [23]

---

[23] http://amix.dk/blog/post/19539

There has been a lot of talk about the aggressive and dominating behavior. According to Fortune "he is considered one of Silicon Valley's leading egomaniacs." There have also been some biographies written about Jobs which also speaks about temperamental issues with him. An authorized biography called "The Little Kingdom" written by Mike Moritz, another one was written by Alan Deutschman titled "The Second Coming of Steve Jobs," and "iCon: Steve Jobs" penned by Jeffrey S. Young & William L. Simon. Steve Jobs was also listed as America's Toughest Bosses by the Fortune magazine for his contribution and leadership of NeXT. Dan Lewin also said that, "The highs were unbelievable, but the lows were unimaginable."

His former partner and colleague, Jef Raskin talked about his personality by saying "Jobs would have made an excellent king of France." Steve Jobs has always tried to develop products which start trends and set examples in front of the industry. He lived with the perception of being innovative in style and technology. He always presented Apple products in his own style and never compromised. After an authorized biography, iCon: Steve Jobs, of Jobs was published by John Wiley & Sons, Apple banned them from Apple Stores.

Steve Jobs has been involved with around 230 patents all related to technology, like computer, and portable consumer devices, etc.

Steve Jobs's wife name is Laurene Powell who he married on March 18, 1991. A Zen Buddhist monk Kobun Chino Otogawa completed the marriage. They have a son, named, Reed Paul Jobs along with two other children. Jobs also had a relationship with Chrisann Brennan, a painter in Bay Area, and he also has a daughter with that relationship named, Lisa Brennan-Jobs who took birth in 1978. Initially, Jobs did not accept the paternity of Lisa explaining that he was on sterile, but accepted it later.

According to an unauthorized biography, "The Second Coming of Steve Jobs," author had written that Jobs had a love connection with Joan Baez. Write talks about Elizabeth Holmes, a friend of Jobs from his time at Reed College, who said that "she believed that Steve became the lover of Joan Baez in large measure because Baez had been the lover of Bob Dylan." According to writers Jeffrey S. Young & William L. Simon, as they had written in "iCon: Steve Jobs" that it is supposed that that Jobs had married Baez who at was of 41 years of age and because of so much difference in age of both, they could not have children.

Jobs also had an altercation with Michael Dell, CEO of Dell, though it was started by Jobs when he talked about Dell creating "un-innovative beige boxes." Later Michael Dell was asked in a Gartner Symposium on October 6, 1997, about Apple, a company troubled with losses, as what he would want to do if he gets an offer, he replied "I'd shut it down and give the money back to the shareholders."

A decade later in 2006, Steve Jobs reminded the Apple employees, as Apple left Dell behind in market shares, through an e-mail. In the e-mail, he wrote: "Team, it turned out that Michael Dell wasn't perfect at predicting the future. Based on today's stock market close, Apple is worth more than Dell. Stocks go up and down, and things may be different tomorrow, but I thought it was worth a moment of reflection today. Steve."[24]

Jobs was diagnosed cancer of pancreases and in the year 2004, he announced about it to his employees, though he said that he has a mild cancerous tumor called islet cell neuroendocrine tumor. He initially emphasized on special diet to fight the disease instead of going for any special medical intervention, though later he agreed to go through pancreaticoduodenectomy which also called Whipple procedure and was performed in July 2004. This procedure excised the tumor successfully and after that he did not receive any chemotherapy or radiation therapy. The head of worldwide sales and operations at Apple, Timothy D. Cook, bore all the responsibilities of Steve Jobs in his absence.

Still, there have been questions raised about his health time to time which he cleared by saying that they are not major concerns and are minimal, but on January 5, 2009, it was reported that Jobs has developed a hormone imbalance disorder and it was said be a serious concern after which he went on a medical leave for six months.

---

[24] http://www.appleinsider.com/articles/06/01/16/apples_jobs_says_michael_dell_should_eat_his_own_words.html

During this time Tim Cook, an acting CEO in 2004, with run the company for the time being while jobs advice will be taken on serious strategic decisions. At Methodist University Hospital Transplant Institute, Jobs went through a liver transplant on April 2009, in Memphis, Tennessee. After the surgery, he recovered well. Jobs returned back to Apple and joined the company again on January 17, 2011.

Jobs has also awarded for his contribution in technology with several renowned like in 1984, he received National Medal of Technology from President Ronald Reagan along with Steve Wozniak and Jefferson Award for Public Service in 1987 for "Greatest Public Service by an Individual 35 Years or Under" also known as "Samuel S. Beard Award" in 1987.

Fortune Magazine named Jobs as the "Most Powerful Person" in business on November 27, 2007. Steve Jobs was also named as the "CEO of the Decade" on November 5, 2009, by Fortune. He was ranked 57th most powerful person by Forbes in November 2009. The Financial Times awarded him with its "Person of The Year" award for 2010.

Computer was named at the "Machine of the Year" by TIME in 1982 and magazine wrote a long article about Steve Jobs, labeling him as "the most famous maestro of the micro." His history and story was also shown in several a film, made about advent of computers and its history, like "Triumph of the Nerds" which came out in 1996, "Nerds 2.0.1" released in 1998, and "Pirates of Silicon Valley" in 1999 which had made about the rise of Apple and Microsoft.

Joshua Schachter
Founder of delicious.com

The 1974 born Joshua Schachter, is the creator of delicious, GeoUrl and has also co-created Memepool. Delicious was the initial site that was created by Joshua in 2003. It is a social bookmarking web service mainly for sharing, storing, and discovering web bookmarks.

In September 2003, Joshua released the first version of the site delicious. com. At that time it was named as del.icio.us. The service of the site was basically based on the term social bookmarking. It also featured tagging, as a system that he developed in support of organizing links recommended to Memepool in addition with publishing a few of them on his personal linkblog, Muxway.

Joshua declared to work on a full time basis for Delicious on March 29, 2005. He devoted most of time and discovered ways to improve the site and worked on each of the details very minutely himself. Yahoo! acquired Delicious on December 9, 2005, the amount at which the acquisition took place was undisclosed. But according to a monthly business magazine, Business 2.0, Yahoo! acquired Delicious for $30 million, with Joshua's share being worth about $15 million. On April 27, 2011, the site was then sold to AVOS Systems.

The site uses a non-hierarchical classification system under which the users can tag each of their bookmarks with the independently chosen index terms which generates a kind of folksonomy. The users can have a combined view about each one's bookmarks with the given tag. The collective nature of the bookmarks makes it feasible to look at the bookmarks added by different other users.

Delicious is one of the most popular social bookmarking services. Many of the features of the site have contributed to its popularity, including human-readable URL scheme, the website's simple interface, a novel domain name, RSS feeds for web syndication and a simple REST-like API. Moreover, use of the site is free. Although the source code of Delicious is not accessible, but users can still download his or her individual data through the site's API in a JSON or XML format, or can even export it to a normal Netscape bookmarks set-up.

All the bookmarks that are posted on the site are openly viewable to everyone by default, though users can still mark definite bookmarks as private, and the bookmarks that are imported are private by default. Delicious is not focused on storing private ("not shared") bookmark collections; the public aspect of the site is paid more attention to. Delicious tagrolls, linkrolls, network badges, the site's daily blog posting feature and RSS feeds can be used to show bookmarks on the web pages.

Before Joshua started to work at Delicious on a full time basis, he used to work as an analyst in the Morgan Stanley's Equity Trading Lab. In 2002, he created GeoURL, and managed it till 2004.

Schachter declared his decision to leave Yahoo! in June 2008. In January 2009, he joined Google and worked there till June 2010. He is also known as a successful angel investor. He made more than 15 investments in the years 2009 and 2010. He invested in several high profile companies like Foursquare, Square, Etsy, Canvas Networks and Bump.

BILL GATES, CO-FOUNDER OF MICROSOFT

It will be really astonishing and perhaps be the greatest charity in the world when one of the richest persons of the world would wish to donate all his wealth for the wellbeing of humanity. It's very difficult to believe that an ambitious and competitive person who earned his wealth with hard work and dedication plans to give away all his wealth for mankind. But this is very true; Bill Gates, Microsoft Chairman, the youngest self-made billionaire of the world declared that he will give away 95% of all his earnings when he will be old and gray.

Bill Gates is an American business magnate, an author, philanthropist and the chairman of Microsoft, the company which he founded along with Paul Allen. Since, 1995 to 2009, only once in the year 2008, he was ranked third amongst the world's wealthiest people. He is being consistent with the numero-uno position as the world's wealthiest person since 1995. Gates held the position of a CEO, all through his career at Microsoft. Along with that, he serves the company as the chief software architect, and he is the largest individual shareholder of the company with 8% of the company stock. Gates is also recognized as an author with several book that he has written himself and co-authored several other.

William Henry "Bill" Gates III was born on October 28, 1955 in Seattle, Washington to William H. Gates, Sr. and Mary Maxwell Gates. He had an upper middle class family background; his father was a famous lawyer and his mother was a member in the board of directors at First Interstate BancSystem and the United Way. His great-grandfather was a state legislator and a mayor. His grandfather was vice president of national bank. He has one elder sister, Kristianne and one younger sister, Libby.

Gates was enrolled at an exclusive preparatory school named Lakeside school at an age of 13. When he was at eighth standard, the Mother's Club used proceeds from the school's rummage sale to buy a block of computer time on a General Electric (GE) computer and an ASR-33 Teletype terminal for the students. He had an excellent record in mathematics and science. During his school days he discovered his interest in software and began programming computers at age of thirteen. From childhood Bill was ambitious, intelligent and competitive. In school Bill and his friends were very much interested in computer and they formed "Programmers Group" and found a new way to apply their computer skill as programmers.

He entered Harvard University for his graduation in 1973 where he met Steve Ballmer, now the chief executive officer of Microsoft. Bill developed a version of the programming language BASIC during his days at Harvard. Gates did not have a distinct study plan at Harvard and used to spent time using the computers.

In January 1975, Gates read the issue of popular electronics in which Altair 8000 was demonstrated. Then he contacted the creators of the new microcomputers, MITS, Micro Instrumentation and Telemetry Systems, just to inform them that he along with others in his group were working on a BASIC interpreter for the platform. But in real Allen and Gates did not had an Altair neither they had written codes for it. Their purpose was to gauge MITS interest in them, and therefore they lied about the fact. Ed Roberts, the president of MITS, agreed to meet them for a demo. In a due course of a few weeks, they developed an Altair emulator that ran on a mini computer. After that they created the BASIC interpreter. Having done that, they demonstrated the whole thing, and the demonstration that they gave at MITS office was a success.

They were able to crack the deal to distribute the interpreter to several distributors as Altair BASIC. In November 1975, MITS hired Paul Allen, and then Gates also took a leave of absence from the Harvard University to work with Allen at MITS in Albuquerque. They named their partnership deal as Micro-soft. The first office of Micro-soft was located at Albuquerque. After one year they dropped the hyphen from the name, and the trade name 'Microsoft' was registered with the Office of the Secretary of the State of Mexico on November 26, 1976. In the due course of time Gates was too much involved with the company and he didn't have the time to return to Harvard. Therefore, he quit Harvard and his studies remained incomplete.

The software that they created Microsoft BASIC was in due time, quite popular amongst the computer hobbyists. Gates soon discovered that a pre-market copy of the software was leaked and was being copied and distributed by the computer hobbyists. Gates wrote an Open Letter to Hobbyists in February, 1976. In the MITS newsletter he announced that MITS could not continue the production and distribution and the maintenance of high quality software without payment. The letter was quite criticized by the computer hobbyists but his idea was that the software developers should get what they are working for and they should get paid from the company they are working with and for whom they are creating new software.

In late 1976, Microsoft became an independent enterprise and separated from MITS. Microsoft after being an independent enterprise continued to work as a software developer and developed programming language software for several other companies. On January 1, 1979, Microsoft shifted its base from Albuquerque to its new destination in Bellevue. During its initial days, all the employees of the company had great responsibility and the company co-operated with them and Bill Gates himself took all the responsibility from writing codes for the company's business. During that time Gates continued to write program codes along with heading all the companies' responsibilities. For the first five years since the company's inception, gates personally reviewed all the codes and scrutinized every line before shipping them and time and again rewrote many of them which he found to be rewritten.

IBM approached Microsoft in 1980, to write the basic interpreter for IBM PC, its forthcoming personal computer. They were in need of an operating system for their computer, when Gates came to know about their need. He referred them to Digital Research (DRI), who was the makers of the extensively used CP/M operating system. But they did not reach the license agreement as the discussion between IBM with Digital Research went poorly. Jack Sams who was then the representative of IBM, explained the licensing difficulties with during a consequent meeting with Gates and asked him to obtain a suitable operating system for their personal computer.

After a few weeks, Gates anticipated using 86-DOS (QDOS), it was an operating system which was similar to CP/M, which Tim Paterson of Seattle Computer Products (SCP) had made for hardware similar to the PC. Thereafter, Microsoft cracked an agreement with SCP to develop into the exclusive licensing mediator, and later on the complete owner, of 86-DOS. Subsequent to adapting the operating system suitably for IBM PC, Microsoft delivered the PC to IBM as PC-DOS in substitute for a once fee which he charged as $50,000. Gates didn't suggest transferring the copyright on that operating system, since he thought that other hardware companies would copy IBM's system. Thereafter, the sales of MS-DOS went higher and made Microsoft a major performer in the software industry.

Bill Gates took the complete responsibility and oversaw Microsoft's company reorganization on June 25, 1981, and once again re-integrated the company in Washington State, in addition to that made Gates President of Microsoft along with being the Chairman of the Board.

On November 20, 1985, Microsoft launched its first retail version of Microsoft Windows, and ion the same year in the month of August; Microsoft cracked a deal with IBM to create an individual operating system and named it as OS/2. Even though both the companies fruitfully developed the initial version of the new operating system, mounting resourceful differences destabilized the partnership. On May 16, 1991, Gates circulated an internal memo, declaring that the OS/2 partnership was finished and Microsoft would swing its efforts towards the progress of Windows NT kernel.

Since, Microsoft's founding in 1975 till the year 2006, Gates had principal liability for Microsoft's product policy. He insistently expanded the company's array of products, and wherever the company achieved a leading position he vigorously secured it. Gates gained a standing for being isolated to others; in 1981 which was not many years after the company was created, an industry executive criticized in public and media that "Gates is notorious for not being reachable by phone and for not returning phone calls".[25]

Being in a supervisory position, Gates met on a regular basis with Microsoft's program managers and senior managers. Immediate accounts of these meetings portray him as orally belligerent, criticizing managers for apparent flaws in their business approach or policies that placed the company's long-standing interests at jeopardy. He time and again interrupted several presentations with comments such as, "Why don't you just give up your options and join the Peace Corps?" and "That's the stupidest thing I've ever heard!" The aim of his comments then had to be defended by the proposal in all the detailed specifics until and unless, Gates was fully persuaded. And whenever his subordinates appeared to be a bit procrastinating, Gates was famous to remark mockingly over them.

Gates' function at Microsoft for the greater part of the history of Microsoft was mainly an executive and management role. Nevertheless, he was a functioning software developer in the initial years, mainly on the Microsoft's programming language products. Gates hasn't formally been on the development team since he last worked on the TRS-80 Model 100, however as late as year 1989 he continued writing codes that shipped in the company's products. Gates announced on June 15, 2006, that he would changeover his everyday role for the next two years to contribute much more time to philanthropy that he considered very important part of his life and existence. He alienated his responsibilities for Microsoft between his two eligible successors, placing Craig Mundie in charge of long-term product strategy and Ray Ozzie in charge of day-to-day management.

In 1975, before graduation Gates left Harvard to form his own company with his childhood friend Paul Allen. The duo planned to develop software for the newly emerging personal computer market. With that thought in mind they began developing software for personal computers and within a year they formed Microsoft. Their vision was "A computer on every desk and Microsoft software on every computer". Their foresight and vision for

---

[25]   http://books.google.com/books?id=rD0EAAAAMBAJ&lpg=PA44&dq=%
22radio%20shack%22%20%22model%20i%22&pg=PA49#v=onepage&
q=%22radio%20shack%22%20%22model%20i%22&f=false

personal computing have been central to the success of Microsoft and the software industry.

For a common man, Microsoft is known for its Windows operating system. Microsoft Windows is a series of operating systems produced by Microsoft. Microsoft first introduced an operating environment named Windows in 1985 as an add-on to MS-DOS in response to the growing demand for graphical user interfaces. Microsoft Windows came to dominate the world's personal computer market. Windows had approximately 91% of the market share of the client operating systems for usage on the Internet. The most recent client version of Windows is Windows 7; the most recent server version is Windows Server 2008 R2 and the most recent mobile version is Windows Phone 7.

Microsoft launched its first retail version of Microsoft Windows in November, 1985, and in August, the company sings a deal with IBM to develop a separate operating system called OS/2. Although the two companies successfully developed the first version of the new system, because of creative differences undermined the partnership. Bill distributed an internal memo in 1991 announcing that the OS/2 partnership with IBM was over and Microsoft would concentrate on its Windows NT kernel development.

Bill Gates is best-known as an entrepreneur of the personal computer revolution. During Microsoft's early years, all employees had broad responsibility for the company's business. Bill Gates used to manage the business at the same time used to write code for complex programs. It's told that during first few years he used to personally review every line of code for the projects and even many of those if he feels not perfect.

Bill stepped down as chief executive officer of Microsoft in January 2000. He remained as chairman and created the position of chief software architect. In June 2006, Bill announced that he would be transitioning from full-time work at Microsoft to part-time work, and full-time work at the Bill & Melinda Gates Foundation. He gradually transferred his duties to Ray Ozzie, chief software architect, and Craig Mundie, chief research and strategy officer. Bill's last full-time day at Microsoft was June 27, 2008. He remains at Microsoft as non-executive chairman.

On January 1, 1994, Bill Gates married Melinda French from Dallas, Texas. They have three children; daughter Jennifer born on 1996, son Rory born on 1999 and daughter Phoebe born on 2002. Bill's home is an earth-sheltered house in the side of a hill overlooking Lake Washington in Medina. His 66,000 sq ft estate has a 60-foot swimming pool with an underwater music system as well as a 2,500 sq ft gym and a 1,000 sq ft dining room.

Amongst Gate's other private acquisitions is a collection of writings by Leonardo da Vinci, the Codex Leicester, which Gates bought at an auction in the year 1994 for $30.8 million. The ceiling of his large home library is engraved with a quotation from The Great Gatsby. According to the King County public records, as of 2006 the entirety assessed worth of the property including his land and house is worth $125 million, and the annual property tax he pays is $991,000.

Bill Gates strongly believes in hard work and dedication. Perhaps these qualities helped him to take Microsoft to the zenith in the software industry. Bill is a person who does not believe in luck but strongly believes in hard work and competitiveness. He likes to play the game of Risk and the game of world domination. Along with that he also enjoys playing tennis, bridge and golf.

Bill Gates ranked first on the Forbes list of The World's Richest People from 1995 to 2007 and 2009 and topped the Forbes 400 list from 1993 through to 2007. Gates' wealth surpassed $101 billion mark, in the year 1999, after which he was considered by the media as a "centibillionaire". After the dot-com bubble burst in 2000, the nominal value of the Microsoft holding declined due to fall in Microsoft's stock prices, and another reason being the multi-billion dollar donations made by him to his charitable foundations.

In May 2006, Gates commented in an interview that he wished he was not the richest man in the world, because he dislikes all the attention that it brought. Along with Microsoft, he has several other investments which provided him with a salary of $616,667 and $350,000 bonus totaling to $966,667 in 2006. He founded a digital imaging company called Corbis, in 1989. He became the director of Berkshire Hathaway, in 2004, the investment company headed by his long-time friend Warren Buffett. In March 2010, Carlos Slim overtook Gates, and became the richest person in the world, while Gate ranked second.

In 1998, the United States v. Microsoft case took place, which led to antitrust litigation over Microsoft's business practices, Gates provided deposition testimony that a number of journalists characterized as ambiguous. He differed with surveyor David Boies over the contextual meaning of words like "compete", "we" and "concerned". Later on Gates said that he had just resisted efforts by Boies to mischaracterize his actions and words. As per his demeanor was concerned during the deposition, he said, "Did I fence with Boies? . . . I plead guilty. Whatever that penalty is should be levied against me: rudeness to Boies in the first degree."[26] In spite of Gates' denial against the violation of Sherman Antitrust Act, the judge ruled that Microsoft had committed tying and monopolization and through these means it has blocked competition.

Since Bill Gates has left Microsoft, he continued with his philanthropy as well as kept himself engaged with other projects, like purchased the video rights of the Messenger Lectures series called The Character of Physical Law, which was given by Richard Feynman in 1964, at Cornell University and recorded by the BBC. Gates was invited to speak at MIT, the Massachusetts Institute of Technology, in April 2010, where he instructed the students to challenge on the difficult problems of the world in their futures

People had great expectations from Bill Gates and they were of the opinion that he should do some charity to help the poor and needy. Therefore, Gates created William H. Gates Foundation in 1994, after selling some of his Microsoft shares. Later on, Gates and his wife joined three foundations to form one Bill & Melinda Gates Foundation in the year 2000. It is the largest most transparently operated charitable trust in the world.

Gates consider David Rockefeller as his inspiration behind being a philanthropist. Gates along with his father have contributed to the Rockefeller family's philanthropic focus, where those social issues are

---

[26]   http://www.wired.com/wired/archive/8.11/microsoft_pr.html

addressed which escapes from the notice of the Government. As per the records of 2007, Gates and his wife ranked second as the most generous philanthropist in America, being donated more than $28 billion as charity.

Bill Gates is charitable person when it comes to computers, internet and any kind of funding. Bill & Melinda Gates Foundation was established in 2000 which used to donate a large amount of money to various charitable organizations and scientific research programs every year. Few years back he visited Chicago's Einstein Elementary School and granted benefiting Chicago's schools and museums where he donated a total of $110,000, a bunch of computers and provided internet connectivity to number of schools. Bill Gates also donated 38 million dollars for the building of a computer institute at Stanford University.

Gates authored the book, Business @ the Speed of Thought, in the year 1999. It is a book that shows how computer technology can solve business problems in fundamentally new ways. It explains us how technology and business are integrated and co-related with each other. It also shows in what way the information networks and the digital infrastructures can help in getting an edge over the competition. Gates through this book has asserted that industry and cyberspace can be no longer considered as separate entities. He is of the opinion and he conveyed it through his book that business model should be modified according to the Information age, if it really wants to succeed.

Although the book is not an entire technology book, but yet it provides us an idea about how to incorporate technology with business process to get the best results out of it and to succeed in the cut throat business environment. It also provides us with the idea as to how a business can make profit with the help of the latest technologies and how development in information technology and networking can bring about a difference in the day to day industry. The book was published in 25 languages and is available in more than 60 countries.

Gates co-authored another book named The Road Ahead, along with Peter Rinearson and Nathan Myhrvold. The book was published in November 1995. The Road Ahead summarizes the suggestions of the personal computing revolution in addition to describing a future profoundly altered by the advent of the global information technology.

Gates got a $ 2.5 million in advance for this book along with money from auxiliary rights sales. Moreover, all his earnings were donated to a foundation created by the National Education Association to "encourage the use of technology in education administered through the National Foundation for the Improvement of Education." After The Road Ahead was written by Gates, but prior to it hitting the bookstores, Gates realized that the Internet was receiving critical mass. Having observed that, on December 7, 1995 only weeks after the book was released—he redirected Microsoft to become an Internet-focused enterprise. Then Gates along with co-author Rinearson spent quite a few months modifying the book and making it 20,000 words longer as well as focused more on the Internet. The revised edition of the book was then published in October 1996 as a trade paperback.

Mutually the editions were published with a CD-ROM that enclosed the text material of the book in addition to the supplemental information. The paperback was provided by Penguin, which was an affiliate of Viking and the hardback was published by Viking themselves. A number of publishers, all over the world created several translated versions of The Road Ahead, which was mainly popular amongst the university students in China.

Nathan Myhrvold, one of the co-authors of The Road Ahead, was a Microsoft vice president and a computer scientist who for a short period of time managed Microsoft's research efforts and afterwards co-founded an intellectual property company, Intellectual Ventures. Whereas, Peter Rinearson, the other co-author, was an entrepreneur and a Pulitzer Prize winner, who later found and sold an Internet company, furthermore became the vice president of Microsoft.

Bill Gates featured in one of the Hollywood movie, Waiting for Superman. It is a documentary film which was released in 2010. The film was directed by Davis Guggenheim and produced by Lesley Chilcott. The title of the film was based on an interview which was held with Geoffrey Canada in which he narrates when he was a child, he was told by his mother that

Superman, the comic super hero, was not real, and was frightened as there was nobody to save him.

Waiting for Superman, received the Best Documentary Feature at the Critics' Choice Movie Awards as well as received the Audience Award for best documentary at the Sundance Film Festival, 2010.

The movie also co-starred, Geoffrey Canada, The Black Family, The Esparza Family, The Hill Family, Bill Strickland, Michelle Rhee, Randi Weingarten, Bill Strickland, Eric Hanushek, Bill Gates and George Reeves as the Superman.

In 2008, Gates appeared in a number of ads for the promotion of his company Microsoft. Two the Microsoft's advertisements co-starred Seinfeld.

Linus Torvalds
Chief Architect of the Linux Kernel

Linus is best known as a Finnish software engineer, who instigated the development of the Linux Operating System and is also its chief architect and project coordinator.

Linus Benedict Torvalds, was born on December 28, 1968 in Helsinki, Finland. His parents are journalist Anna and Nils Torvalds, and he is the grandson of the famous poet Ole Torvalds. He was named after the American Nobel Prize winning chemist, Linus Pauling. Since, his childhood he had great interest in computers. In 1996, Linus Torvalds graduated with a master's degree in Computer Science from the University of Helsinki. While he was in college, he joined the Finnish army. He spent almost a year receiving the military training and also retains the rank of second lieutenant. He again resumed and continued with his studies from the year 1990.

Torvalds bought his first personal computer in the year 1987. But still the operating system and the programmes failed to interest him, therefore, he began to build his own operating system from the scratch and the result was the birth of Linux. It was based on the combination of MINIX and UNIX. He was first exposed to UNIX, in the form of a DEC MicroVAX running ULTRIX.

With a Commodore VIC-20, he began experimenting with his interest in computers. His next step towards his love for computers was buying a Sinclair QL. He modified his QL extensively, and mostly its operating system. Torvalds, programmed a text editor, along with an assembly language and few other games, for the QL. Torvalds purchased an Intel 80386-based IBM PC, on January 5, 1991. He used his new PC mostly for playing games, before he got his MINIX copy, which helped him to further his work on his own operating system, Linux.

About the naming of the operating system, there were several speculations. At first, Torvalds wanted to name the Kernel that he developed as Freax, the name symbolized and was the combination of free, freak and MINIX. However, Torvald's friend Ari Lemmke, who was also the administrator of the FTP server, where the operating system was initially hosted for downloading, suggested the name Linux for the directory. Linus Torvalds released the primary version of his operating system Linux in the year 1991.

Torvald started working with Transmeta Corporation, and then after few years moved to the Open Source Development Labs. The company then merged with the Free Standards Group to form the Linux Foundation. Since 1997 till 1999 he was occupied with 86open assisting in choosing the binary format for UNIX as well as Linux. Big companies like VA Linux and Red Hat, both foremost developers of Linux based software, offered Torvalds, stock options in lieu for his creation of the operating system. For this reason both the companies went public about their opinion in the year 1999 as a result, the value of his shares shot up to approximately $20 million.

Linux Kernel is amongst the most appropriate examples of free and open space software. Under the GNU General Public License version 2 (GPLv2) license, the kernel was released, and it was developed by worldwide contributors. In the Linux Kernel mailing list, the day-to-day development and discussion takes place. Soon after its inception Linux accumulated users and developers who modified codes and adapted them from other free software sources to use them in the new operating system.

As per the reports, till the year 2006, about 2 % of the kernel was primarily written by Torvalds himself. Where thousands of people have contributed codes for the development of Linux kernel, this is quite a high percent, and accounts to one of the highest personal contributions amongst the overall number of codes. Torvalds is the ultimate authority, and makes all the decision as to what new codes should be incorporated and what not into the standard Linux operating system. Torvalds is the owner of the

'Linux Trademark' and its use is chiefly monitored by the Linux Mark Institute.

Linux version 0.01 was released by September 1991; it was uploaded on the FTP server of the Helsinki University of Technology (HUT). At that point of time, it had only 10,239 lines of code. Linux version 0.02 was released in October 1991. Linux 0.11 was released on December 1991. This version was one of the first to be self-hosted and it could be compiled by computer running on Linux 0.11. The earlier released versions did not had the GNU General Public License (GPL), therefore were not permitted commercial redistribution. But the next version Linux 0.12 which was released in February 1992, for that Torvalds adopted the GNU General Public License which was previously self-drafted.

Torvalds started a newsgroup called as *alt.os.linux*, and the first post to alt.os.linux was made on 19 January 1992. alt.os.linux became *comp.os.linux* on 31 March 1992.

Soon, the X Window System was ported to Linux. Linux version 0.95 was the primary to be able to run X, in March 1992. There was a large version jump from 0.1x to 0.9x, and this was done intentionally to develop a feeling that the upcoming version 1.0 was imminent with no major missing pieces. But this somewhat proved to be over optimistic and 15 development versions of version 0.99 appeared from 1993 to early 1994. And thereafter, Linux 1.0.0 was released on 14 March 1994, with 176,250 lines of code. Linux 1.2.0 was released in March 1995, with 310,950 lines of code.

In July 2009, the Hyper-V drivers were submitted to the kernel by Microsoft, which enhanced the performance and the activities of virtual Linux guest system in the Windows hosted environment. When it was learnt that Microsoft had integrated a Hyper-V network driver with GPL-licensed components statically linked to closed-source binaries, it was forced to submit the code.

The mascot of the Linux kernel is a penguin, named as Tux, which is also Torvald's personal mascot.

As per Torvalds personal life, he got married to Tove Torvalds, who is a six time Finnish national karate champion. He is a father of three daughters, Patricia Miranda (5.12.1996), Daniela Yolanda (16.4.1998), and Celeste Amanda (20.11.2000). Linus and Tove met during the autumn of 1993. While Linus was conducting an introductory computer laboratory exercise for the students, he asked the course attendants to send him a test mail, as a respond to which, Tove sent him a test mail asking him for a date. Later on they fell in love and got married and are parents of three daughters.

Torvalds considers himself to be a complete atheist. He is of the view that religion actually distracts from both morals as well as the love for nature. He also criticizes the politicized outlook over the religious matter which is mostly common in America, and is of the view that religion is a completely personal matter and should not be used as a division between people and states.

Although, Torvalds is registered as a voter and have the right to vote in the United States, he is independent of any political party and openly disassociates himself with any of the U.S. political parties. As per the academics is concerned, in the year 1997, Linus received his Master's degree in the department of Computer science, from the University of Helsinki. Just after two years, i.e. in 1999, he received an honorary status of doctorate at the Stockholm University and in the year 2000, he received the doctorate status for his *alma mater*. Torvalds received the Vollum Award from the Reed College, in August, 2005.

Linus Torvalds is also a proud recipient of several awards for industrial excellence. He received the prestigious EFF Pioneer Award in 1998. The British Computer Society awarded him with the Lovelace Medal, in the year 2000. Just after one year, Torvalds received the Takeda Awards for Social and Economic Well-Being, which he shared with Ken Sakamura and Richard Stallman.

He was introduced in the Hall of Fellows at the Computer History Museum in Mountain View, California, in the year 2008, and in 2010 he received the C&C Prize, which was awarded by the NEC Corporation, for his "contributions to the advancement of the information technology industry, education, research, and the improvement of our lives"[27].

Many a time, Torvalds has been recognized and honored by the media as well. According to the Time Magazine, he ranked 17th in the Time 100: The Most Important People of the Century poll. In the year 2004, he was recognized as one amongst the few most influential people in the world. And soon after two years, in 2006, Time Magazine's Europe edition considered Torvalds as one of the revolutionary heroes in the past 60 years.

The InfoWorld awarded him with the 2000 award for industry Achievement. In a survey conducted by the BusinessWeek, Torvalds was recognized amongst "the best managers", in the year 2005. He was named one amongst the "10 people who don't matter" by the Business 2.0 magazine, considering the fact that the growth of Linux has decreased Torvalds' individual influence.

Linus Torvalds has several other honors to his name, one of the most eminent being an asteroid, 9793 Torvalds, named after him in the year 1996.

Most recently, in March 2011, he was honored with 35 patents worldwide.

---

27   http://www.h-online.com/open/news/item/Linus-Torvalds-awarded-2010-C-C-Prize-1122542.html

GARRETT GRUENER FOUNDER AND DAVID WARTHEN CO-FOUNDER OF ASK.COM

GARRETT GRUENER

Garrett Gruener is a venture capitalist plus an entrepreneur. With more than three decades of experience under his belt, Garrett Gruener the founder of Ask.com is all set in the fields of system engineering, software development and corporate development. Garrett is also the co-founder of Alta, and along with it he even partnered at Burr, Egan, Deleage & Co., which was joined by him in the year 1992.

Garrett founded the famous search engine Ask Jeeves, now Ask.com, in the year 1996, along with David Warthen as a co-founder. The search engine is now also a part of the IAC. The original software for the search engine was implemented and designed by Gary Chevsky. Around the core search engine, Chevsky, Warthen, Justin Grant and a few others assisted in building the website, AskJeeves.com, which was an earlier version of the search engine we know now.

Building the search engine was a great responsibility and three big venture capital firms namely Institutional Venture Partners, The RODA Group and Highland Capital Partners were the early investors who invested their capital to launch the website. InterActiveCorp is the current owner of the website Ask.com, and is under the NASDAQ symbol IACI.

The search engine outsourced its web search technology to a third party company and remained restrained as a question-answer site after facing a strong competition from the widely used search engine Google in the later half of 2010.

The language used in the website was considered to be natural, everyday use language which was easy to understand and the users could ask any sort of question related to any topic and get the answers from the website. It supported students as well, along with keyword search; they could find assistance on subjects with features like dictionary, math and other conversion questions.

In the year 2005, the name of the website changed from AskJeeves.com to ask.com, the U.K. and Ireland version of the site was named as uk.ask.com. Some of the corporate details of the website are as follows: Since July 1999 till July 2005, Ask Jeeves, Inc. traded their stock on the NASDAQ stock exchange, under the symbol of ASKJ. But after the acquisition of the company by InterActiveCorp, in July 2005, ASKJ stock retired at a value of $1.85 billion.

Garrett did his Bachelors in Science from the University of California, San Diego and Master's degree from the University of California, Berkeley.

Along with a few of his venture capital companies, Garrett also participated in the 2003 California recall, which is special election from the Democratic Party. Out of 135 candidates, he ranked 28th in the field with 2,562 votes. Garrett specialized in the Information technology. He is also one of the members in the board of directors of nCircle Network Security and Aegis security. He is also serving as an acting CEO in Xelerated and Nanomix.

Garrett is married to attorney Amy Slater, and they reside in Berkley with their daughter Dakota Gruener.

David Warthen

David Warthen was born on December 10, 1957. He is well-known as the Co-founder of Ask Jeeves along with Garrett Gruener. He is a pioneer in Engineering and has been associated with creating and developing innovative software technology for more than two decades. He is famous as the co-founder of Ask Jeeves, now Ask.com along with being its Chief Technology officer [CTO].

Warthen along with Garrett is responsible for establishing the first of its kind natural language search engine existing in the virtual world. They created and conceptualized the search engine with user friendly interface, and user centric approach to retrieve information and queries in a useful and easy manner.

The search engine AskJeeves.com, was a success and it grew to develop into one amongst top fifteen internet sites. David Warthen was the one responsible for piloting the company through its initial stages till it became a success story, and now as we all know it is a well established website and answers over 3 million questions everyday, and during peak traffic period it even has a record of answering more than 5 million questions a day.

Currently David Warthen is the founder and the CEO of Future Vistas, Inc. It is a technology innovation firm based in Berkley, which renders development consulting services and technical research. Future Vistas, Inc. is associated with thorough internal research and development, and its main area of focus being grid computing, search and information retrieval software and bio-informatics. Along with this, Warthen is also associated with the economic, societal and the legal proposition of technological application.

Before Warthen started working with Future Vistas, he was working at GlobalStreams, Inc., in the post of a Chief Technology officer [CTO]. It was a pioneering, digital video processing corporation with 100 employees. There he directed the development of company's principal products OnQ and Globecaster. These were the all-in-one software which was involved with meeting the requirements and specified needs of corporate, education and broadcast clients in the vast market which was open and quite emerging for video market which was streaming at that time.

Warthen received his bachelor's degree in both Biology and computer Science from the University of California at San Diego in the year 1981. Since then, he began his career and started working on new projects related to information and technology. Then he started working as a programmer for NCR before he moved to Berkley to join Virtual Microsystems, which was a venture-funded startup, in the year 1983. Since, then he developed from a programmer to becoming the Vice President of engineering in just six years time period. Being associated with the aforesaid company, Warthen along with few other engineers produced pioneering multi-processor hardware and software and co-processor that allowed VAX computers to run DOS applications.

During 1980s, he worked on multiple avant-garde technical aspects such as on PC emulation and ROM BIOS, on fast mini-computer device drivers, network protocols, multi-processor operating system technology and so on. He worked on different cutting edge technological issues and made great advancement for the next generation to benefit from it.

After many years of autonomous consulting, in 1990, Warthen established a software development outsourcing company, Desktop Software which was based on Berkley itself. There he was responsible for managing a team of engineers to implement a file system, networking protocols, as well as CD-ROM servers for their clients, who were the big names of the IT industry including, multi-processor operating system technology, Quantum, Logicraft, LanTec, Microsoft and others. He was also interested and therefore studied information retrieval technology, while he was working on the CD-ROM server applications. He even laid his hands on the development of a Florida, Orlando-based Time Warner ITV trials interactive television channel.

In the year 1995, Warthen formed a partnership with Garrett Gruner, who was a venture capitalist and the ex-CEO of Virtual Microsystems, to form and develop the ground-breaking idea of a search engine. They both worked upon the idea and formed Ask Jeeves, Inc., later known as ask. com, in the year 1996.

During the tenure of Warthen, the search engine developed through leaps and bounds from a mere trial product in 1995 to a world acclaimed IPO in just a few years time. This was majorly because of its user friendly attributes and efficient, easy-to-implement output, that during 1990s it outperformed all other existing search engine sites and became one of the leading search engines with respect to customer satisfaction.

The technology used by the search engine was privately licensed and also used on personalized, domain-specific applications on more than a hundred corporate web sites, which includes, Daimler Chrysler, American Express, Hewlett Packard, Visa, Dell Computers, along with the state of Washington.

Warthen is a regular speaker on search technologies and information retrievals and he still continues to be a part of national as well as international conferences related to these subjects. At present he is working towards research in computing and graduate work at the school of Information Management and Systems (SIMS) at the University of California at Berkley. He even founded a web cam based video game company, Eye Games in the year 2004.

Warthen tied the knot with a Stanford Law School graduate, Cristina Schultz, in April 2004. She is also an alleged former escort and a fitness model. On January 2009, both filed a divorce.

CATERINA FAKE
AND STEWART BUTTERFIELD
FOUNDERS OF FLICKR.COM

STEWART BUTTERFIELD

Daniel Stewart Butterfield is an entrepreneur and businessman. He was born in the year 1973, in a town called Lund, British Columbia. He received the undergraduate degree from University of Victory in Philosophy. He went on to complete his graduation in cognitive science, philosophy of mind and philosophy of biology from the Cambridge University in England. Thereafter, he also did his master's in philosophy from the same institution.

After completing his studies, Stewart returned back to British Columbia and settled in Vancouver, where he worked for several large companies as a web design consultant and a computer programmer. He along with his wife Caterina Fake founded the mother company Ludicorp and developed a photo sharing website named Flickr.com.

Stewart proposed Fake to start a venture with him, even before he asked her for marriage. The idea of starting something exciting which would keep the netizens occupied was already in their mind. Just after two weeks of their honeymoon, they started their new venture in the year 2002. The Vancouver-based company was finally launched in February, 2004.

The idea was to create a web based, multiplayer online game, *Game Neverending*, but the idea of developing Flickr.com, a photo sharing website seemed more feasible, and therefore, the company morphed into a photo sharing website and in no time became one of the most famous sites in the virtual world. And the idea of the multiplayer online game was finally shelved.

While creating Flickr, both its founder thought of creating a gaming site which would not only interest the young generation but also the adults. But eventually it stood up to become the favorite photo sharing site in the web world. In March, 2005, Yahoo purchased Flickr for $35 million. Within a few days all the contents of the website got migrated to servers in United States from Canada, and ultimately they were subjected to United States federal law. Along with a structural and design overhaul, Flickr got updated from beta to gamma version, on May 16, 2006.

Eventually in June 2007, Yahoo! made Flickr their sole and elite photo sharing website shutting down Yahoo photos. And today the website hosts more than 2 billion images. Yahoo! acquired Ludicorp and employed Butterfield as the General Manager of the company. Butterfield left Yahoo! on July 12, 2008. And just the next year in 2009, he founded another gaming startup, Tiny Speck.

Flickr.com is not only serving as a photo sharing website, but is also helping a huge number of bloggers to help upload their photos that they embed in social networks and blogs. 20 megabytes of space was offered to the Flickr users and a month of free access as well, in which you can host 10 to 25 pictures for free, or users could also sign up for an annual fee of $24.95.

Flickr is now also a part of important apps in mobile devices, like iPhone and other smartphones, Windows Phone 7 and BlackBerry. Now you can directly click a photo through your mobile phone and host it on the web through this application. Moreover, because of its easy to use, user-friendly interface and easy upload techniques Flickr became very famous amongst the young generation.

The earlier version of the website was mainly focused on FlickrLive, a multiuser chat room with real time photo exchange features. Then after sometime it became solely an image hosting site and the chat room was eventually dropped. Some of the features that you can see now but were absent previously are, marking photos as favorites, tagging the photos with the name of your friend, interestingness and group photo pools, the founders are still waiting to receive patents on that.

CATERINA FAKE

Catrina Fake is a Filipino-American born on June 13, 1969, at Pittsburgh, Pennsylvania. She is of Filipino and German descent. Fake studied at a private school in Connecticut, Choate Rosemary Hall, she then went on to get her undergraduate degree from Smith College, Massachusetts, and in 1991, and she earned a literature degree from Vassar College. For the next three years, she worked as an assistant to a painter, in an investment bank.

In 1994, she shifted to San Francisco, and worked for a number of web based companies and eventually found her place as an art director of an online magazine, named Salon.com. Caterina.net was her personal site and one of the first "blogs" or web logs to gain a prominent place and a number of followers on the internet, amongst whom Butterfield who later became her husband was an ardent follower.

Fake and Butterfield first met in the year 2000 at a party held at San Francisco, where Butterfield asked her for a date, which she turned down as she was already involved romantically with Evan Williams. But as Fake and Williams parted ways, which was declared by her through her official site, Butterfield again asked her for a date, which she accepted. He invited her to come to British Columbia and enjoy skiing with him. It was during that trip when he suggested that both of them should together create a website. Later on they got married. Fake is four years older to her husband Butterfield. On July 10, 2007, they were the parents of a baby girl. They named them Sonnet Beatrice Butterfield.

In 2001, Fake relocated to Vancouver, and they started their own company Ludicorp. It was a small low investment company specially designed for multi9player online video game called Game Neverending. But instead they developed a unique photo hosting website, which they never thought would be such a path breaking idea. Within a few months Flickr's popularity topped the charts with a huge number of registered users and millions of photos being posted on the website. The idea of Flickr.com was such a hit that they shelved their plans of the Game Neverending and concentrated completely on Flickr.

From an art director, Fake turned into a marketing whiz, just by applying the novel idea of uploading photos on the web through Flickr.com. Fake, along with husband Stewart Butterfield, hatched the idea of uploading photo on the web without much hassle and difficulty. Both of them started Flickr.com in February, 2004, and till then it has grown in leaps and bounds with about three million registered users and about 130 million photos uploaded through the site. Both initiated with the idea and without any money invested in the process. Now Flickr is a well known name and is up there to stay.

Fake is currently serving as a Chief Product Office at Hunch. She is a business women and an entrepreneur and along with that she is a board member and Chairman at Etsy.com. At Founder Collectives, she is a Founder Partner and she even advises several new businesses and start-up companies. After Yahoo! acquired Flickr, she was responsible for the Technology Development Group at Yahoo; she even ran the hack Yahoo program and founded Yahoo's Brickhouse. On June 13, 2008, Fake resigned from Yahoo.

Along with venturing into so many enterprises she is also deeply involved in the expansion of social software, online community and personal publishing. In August, 2008, she joined the Creative Commons as a member of the Board of Directors. She received an Honorary Doctorate from the Rhode Island School of Design on May, 2009.

Fake has received several awards, which include Forbes 2005 eGang, BusinessWeek's Best Leaders of 2005, Red Herring's 20 Entrepreneurs under 35 and Fast Company's Fast 50 award. In 2006, she appeared in the cover page of Newsweek and was named amongst the Time Magazine's list of the world's 100 most influential people.

Fake currently resides in California, New York and San Francisco.

STEVE HUFFMAN
CO-FOUNDER OF REDDIT.COM

Steve Huffman was born on November 12, 1983. He graduated from the University of Virginia, and soon after at an early age of 22, he founded Reddit.com with Alexis Ohanian. In the recent past, Huffman has co-founded the airfare hunt site Hipmunk. They started the company in the year 2005, with initial funding done by Y Combinator. Since, their college days both the founders wanted to start their venture in the internet. Therefore Reditt.com was born.

Huffman and Alexis lived together at the age of 22, when they thought of starting a new venture. The story of Reddit is no different from any other start-up companies. But the kind of devotion that the partners showed while creating the site, is worth mentioning. Since the idea of creating the website came into their mind, both the partners stated breathing and even living their dream. Both of them took a train from UVA to Boston with the intension to hear the Paul Graham talk on How to start a start up. They got inspired by the show and joined the first batch of Y Combinator in spring of 2005 at Boston.

Reddit was started as a social news website. In no time Reddit was a success. And it was acquired by Condé Nast Digital, which is a subsidiary of Advance Magazine Publishers Inc., on October 31, 2006. Since then, Reddit has become a household name.

The site was founded by Steve Huffman and Alexis Ohanian. In 2005 the team expanded and Aaron Swartz and Christopher Slowe were included in the team. The company merged with Swartz's Infogami in late January. As a result of company's merger Aaron Swartz joined the company. On

October 31, 2006, soon after the owner of Wired, Condé Nast Publications, acquired Reddit the consequence was Swartz was fired.

The users of the site have the option to submit links related to any kind of news, or there are also other categories where they can contribute links and contents. While other users have the option to vote the posted links as 'up' or 'down', and the one which receives the most number of ups, tops the chart and appears in the front page.

In addition to that, the users can also post their comments related to the posts as well as reply to the comments of other users. And thereby, they are able to form an online community of their own. The Reddit users also have the provision to create their own sections, referred to as sub-reddits section. These sections are created for a specific niche and the users can create their own community through it as well as posts their comments on that. The appearance of the posts on the website's front page is also determined by several other factors like the age of the post submitted, the total vote count and the positive or negative feedback.

The users can also customize the submissions which appear on the front page. They can also modify these posts and post them in another website. A number of submissions rotate through the front page on a daily basis. The site also contains an area for discussion, in which users may even discuss with other users and can vote for or against other people's comment as well. By default, the post which gets the most popular comment rises on the top. Whereas, the posts in which there are maximum negative comments are not displayed on the site. The discussion area of the site is particularly very active as per the June 2011 reports and regularly generates hundreds of comments per submission. This process has been able to generate several memes inside the Reddit community.

The various sections of the community are: Programming, Atheism, Science, Pics, Politics, Gaming, World News, Trees, and AskReddit. Users have the option to customize which page they want as their front page in the website. They can change their appearance of the site according to their wish.

Reddit became an open source project On June 18, 2008. All the codes and libraries of the site became freely available on Github, with exceptions of the anti-spam/cheating portions.

Reddit was named in Lead411's "2010 Hottest San Francisco Companies" list, in May 2010.

Huffman met Katie, now his wife, in college. But their relationship was not a bed of roses. That time they couldn't devote much time together because he was too much involved with the work for his new website. Steve says "Alexis and I were in Boston for the summer of the first YC batch, and we thought we'd be coming back to Virginia after that. Then Paul Graham convinced us to stay. We had actually signed a lease in Virginia, and had to wiggle our way out. That was a really tough conversation with Katie. She was pretty upset, when we decided to stay in Boston. We ended up being long-distance for quite a while."[28]

Huffman and his partner Alexis worked really hard and their hard slog paid off when Reddit was acquired by Condé Nast Digital just after one year of its launch. Thereafter the duo, moved to San Francisco to work at the Condé Nast's wired office. Though the deal was quite supportive for their venture, but they had a three years of agreement in which they could not leave the company. Whereas, he wanted to get back to work for his next startup, where he could work independently on tricky problems with the support of the community of hackers. He reflects that, "Condé Nast didn't have that, and that made it tough. I was frustrated because I felt like I wasn't learning anymore. We were still trying to do new things, but the bigger you are the harder that is. There were some challenging policies there. Certainly if you're a tech company, it's almost impossible to function within a non-tech company, because they just don't get it."[29]

He was quite bewildered with the decisions that he had to make for his personal life. He wanted to get back to Virginia, but was handcuffed with Condé Nast, and his fiancé Katie was in medical school in Virginia, which made their relationship more difficult. He had the intensions to

---

[28] http://meetthefounders.com/meet-steve-huffman-cofounder-of-reddit-and-hi
[29] http://meetthefounders.com/meet-steve-huffman-cofounder-of-reddit-and-hi

do another startup, and had plans to relocate back to Virginia and get married to Katie.

In October 2009, Huffman left Reddit and got married to Katie. That time, Katie had one year of studies still left to be completed. He took advantage of it and used the time to think about his next venture. This time he had three years of experience under his belt and his vision this time was very sturdy as to what he really wanted to do. That time he got in touch with Adam Goldstein, who later on became his co-partner. They met at the Foo Camp during the summer, soon after Reddit was launched, and since then they have been friends and stayed together. They started a new airfare search website Hipmunk.

JEFF GOLD FOUNDER OF GO.COM

Jeff is a business consultant who provides business start-ups, management, financial, marketing and merger and acquisition advice and consulting. Jeff through his expertise, helps to prepare business plans to assist new business succeed and obtain financing. He has been an entrepreneur over the past 24 years. He has been successfully launching numerous well known brands and started ten of his own business. Amongst them several were acquired by very reputed major corporations.

Nathan Gold is the father of Jeff and is known for his inventions. His father invented and secured United States and international patents for several of his well known inventions including: digital fax machines, recordable CDs (CD-R), Polaroid instant cameras and electronic flash photography. Jeff learned many of his creative, technical and problem solving techniques from his father.

Jeff himself was awarded full-tuition scholarships by the University of Southern California, U.C. Santa Barbara and U.C.L.A. In 1981, he secured the first position in a Math competition which was offered to students throughout California by U.C. Santa Barbara. In 1983, he was recognized by the U.C.L.A. Alumni Scholarship Program.

Jeff founded 10 businesses of his own which includes, Q Network (Q.com), Q.com was acquired by Qwest Communications, whereas Q network, which is the provider of Web site services to more than 3000 radio & TV stations, newspapers and magazines was acquired by Mainstream Capital.

He also found 100 Top Network, Go.com (which is one of the first entertainment portals in the internet and was acquired by the Walt Disney Company), World Environmental Organization, FM Net, GoTo.

com (it was acquired by idealab!), Classroom Computer Company (it was acquired by Educational Acquisition Corp.), Cyberlearn, A Lasting Impression Corp., Double-Gold Software, Inc and FastAccess.com which was acquired by Bell South.

Along with creating and running new enterprises and his own businesses, Jeff spends quite a few hours every week with the small business owners as well as executives of large companies over the phone and guide them and advice them how to run their businesses.

Jeff also helps the startups by providing them with an effective business plan. He thinks that the foundation of a strong business lays in a strong business plan. He helps the small businesses to create a professional business plan that will help them to lay a stronger foundation stone to make their business sturdy and successful. He advises the small business owners in creating such business plans that will help them to attract the interest of investors and bankers.

Jeff also gives the startup enterprise advice of how to test market a product or service before actually launching it into the bigger market. His opinion in this matter is that, it is very important to test market a product by fine-tuning the new item prior to bringing them in the mass market. Therefore, he shows them how to do that effectively and quickly. He also recommends the small businesses how to save each dollar and thereby earn profit through it. Effective cost negotiation is very important to generate profit in the small business startup therefore,

Jeff Gold is the founder of The Go Network, now Go.com. It is a web portal launched in 1995.

Niklas Zennström, Janus Friis and Samuel Gray, Co-founders of Skype

Skype was founded by Janus Friis from Denmark, Samuel Gray from New Jersey and Niklas Zennström from Swedenn in 2003. Priit Kasesalu, Jaan Tallinn and Estonians Ahti Heinla, together developed the software for Skype. They were also the developer of the Kazaa, which is the peer-to-peer file sharing software. The Skype.net and Skype.com domain names were registered in April, 2003. The initial beta version of the software was released in August, 2003. The name Skype was derived from the initial name of the project, which was "Sky peer-to-peer", Then the founders decided to abbreviate the name as "Skyper", but this domain name was already registered by someone else. Therefore, they thought of dropping the 'r' from the name and the name 'Skype' was then finalized and registered.

Skype is well known as the software application, which allows its users to make video and voice calls and chat over the internet, The service is for free, unlike the services of landlines and mobile phones, which charges a fee for making calls. Huge numbers of users are using Skype as an alternative to phone, mostly for making international calls.

There are also additional features associated which the site, for example, file transfer, video conferencing and instant messaging. As per the reports of 2010, Skype had 663 million registered users.

Skype limited, operates its services, from its headquarters situated at Luxembourg. There are offices of Skype at Tartu and Tallinn, Estonia, where most of the Skype development team and almost 44 per cent of the employees of Skype are situated.

Skype is not like the other VoIP services, rather than a client server system, it is a peer-to-peer system. It uses the background processing technique on computers running on Skype software. That is the reason why the system was named as Sky-peer-to-peer in its initial stage.

Skype have been banned in some corporate offices, education networks, government sectors and home due to its excessive bandwidth usage, inappropriate usage of resources and due to security concerns.

Microsoft Corporation acquired Skype Communications on 10 May, 2011, for US$8.5 billion. Microsoft acquired all the technologies, including Skype, and together it will be incorporated as a division of Microsoft.

The registered users of the site are identified with unique Skype names and listed in the Skype directory. The registered users can communicate with both voice chat and instant messaging services through Skype.

Voice chat facilitates telephone calls among pairs of users as well as conference calling, along with a proprietary audio codec. The software's text chat allows the clients to do group chats, use emoticons, saving and storing chat history, and offline messaging along with editing of earlier messages. The general features similar to instant messaging—online status indicators, user profiles, and so on—are also incorporated.

Video conferencing between two users was introduced in January 2006 for the Windows and Mac OS X platform clients. Skype 2.0 for Linux, released on 13 March 2008, also features support for video conferencing. Version 5 beta 1 for Windows, released 13 May 2010, offers free video conferencing with up to five people.

The Online Number, named as SkypeIn, service facilitaes Skype users to dial and receive calls on their computers dialed by regular phone subscribers to a local Skype phone number; local numbers are accessible for Belgium, Brazil, Chile, Australia, Colombia, the Dominican Republic, Estonia, Denmark, Germany, Hong Kong, Finland, France, Hungary, Ireland,

New Zealand, Poland, Italy, Japan, Mexico, Romania, South Africa, the Netherlands, the United Kingdom, South Korea, Sweden, Switzerland, and the United States. A Skype user can as well have local numbers in any of these countries, with calls to the number charged at the same rate as calls to fixed lines in the country. Skype is truly regarded as the next generation technology that has become the need for the hour.

SkypeOut was restricted in China, In September 2005. Same year in October, eBay purchased the company for 2.6 billion dollars. (In 2011, the Ars Technica calculated the purchase amount at $3.1 billion, and not $ 2.6 billion.) The videotelephony was introduced in December 2005,.

Skype for Windows, beginning with version 3.6.0.216, supports "High Quality Video" with quality and features, *e.g.*, full-screen and screen-in-screen modes, similar to those of mid-range videoconferencing systems. Skype audio conferences currently support up to 25 people at a time, including the host.

Skype does not provide the ability to call emergency numbers such as 911 in the United States and Canada, 999 in the United Kingdom and many other countries, 111 in New Zealand, 000 in Australia, or 112 in Europe. The U.S. Federal Communications Commission (FCC) has ruled that, for the purposes of section 255 of the Telecommunications Act, Skype is not an "interconnected VoIP provider". As a result, the U.S. National Emergency Number Association recommends that all VoIP users have an analog line available as a backup.

In 2011, Skype partnered with Comcast to bring its video chat service to Comcast subscribers via their HDTV sets

Registered users of Skype are identified by a unique Skype Name, and may be listed in the Skype directory. Skype allows these registered users to communicate through both instant messaging and voice chat. Voice chat allows telephone calls between pairs of users and conference calling, and uses a proprietary audio codec. Skype's text chat client allows group chats, emoticons, storing chat history, offline messaging (since version 5) and editing of previous messages. The usual features familiar to instant messaging users—user profiles, online status indicators, and so on—are also included.

The Online Number, a.k.a. SkypeIn, service allows Skype users to receive calls on their computers dialed by conventional phone subscribers to a local Skype phone number; local numbers are available for Australia, Belgium, Brazil, Chile, Colombia, Denmark, the Dominican Republic, Estonia, Finland, France, Germany, Hong Kong, Hungary, Ireland, Italy, Japan, Mexico, New Zealand, Poland, Romania, South Africa, South Korea, Sweden, Switzerland, the Netherlands, the United Kingdom, and the United States. A Skype user can have local numbers in any of these countries, with calls to the number charged at the same rate as calls to fixed lines in the country.

Video conferencing between two users was introduced in January 2006 for the Windows and Mac OS X platform clients. Skype 2.0 for Linux, released on 13 March 2008, also features support for video conferencing. Version 5 beta 1 for Windows, released 13 May 2010, offers free video conferencing with up to five people.

Skype for Windows, starting with version 3.6.0.216, supports "High Quality Video" with quality and features, e.g., full-screen and screen-in-screen modes, similar to those of mid-range videoconferencing systems. Skype audio conferences currently support up to 25 people at a time, including the host.

Skype does not provide the ability to call emergency numbers such as 911 in the United States and Canada, 999 in the United Kingdom and many other countries, 111 in New Zealand, 000 in Australia, or 112 in Europe. The U.S. Federal Communications Commission (FCC) has ruled that, for the purposes of section 255 of the Telecommunications Act, Skype is not an "interconnected VoIP provider". As a result, the U.S. National Emergency Number Association recommends that all VoIP users have an analog line available as a backup.

In 2011, Skype partnered with Comcast to bring its video chat service to Comcast subscribers via their HDTV sets.